This page is intentionaly left blank.

UNDER A ZAMBIAN TREE

DORA MOONO NYAMBE'S QUEST TO EDUCATE HER NATION

JOSEPH SCHMITT

FOREWORD BY DORA MOONO NYAMBE

Published by Great Lakes Publishing

Manufactured in the United States of America

Library of Congress Control Number: 2023901293

ISBN 979-8-9874319-2-4

ISBN 979-8-9874319-1-7 (pbk)

ISBN 979-8-9874319-0-0 (ebook)

Dedication

This book is dedicated to the students at Footprints of Hope.

Contents

Foreword by Dora Moono Nyambe

I would like each reader to know that everything in this book is very real. The experiences described were much more graphic and raw in person than can possibly be explained. During the interview stage I opened up immensely. This at times was a difficult and painful process. It took enormous trust to let another person into my life. Joseph Schmitt was able to see beyond the curated narrative I share online and understand what drives me. Now I am embarking on another emotional challenge, letting you, the reader, into this planet.

The story you are about to read has been many years in the making. The author of the book, Joseph Schmitt, is someone I have come to know closely. To have a written account of what I and others have accomplished in Mapapa is an astonishing achievement. It takes a special person to come to a remote village and interact on other people's level. Joseph's intuition and acknowledgment of the dignity of those he encountered was evident through his actions. Our relationship enabled this story to be told in the most respectful way possible. Joseph's involvement as a narrator is essential in communicating many of the unspoken and raw moments of my journey. I know that what he experienced along with me had a deep impact on his perspectives and writing. I am thankful for his kindness and ability to extend himself to great lengths to put our story into words.

Footprints of Hope is still early in its journey, and I envision much more in its future. I know that we are having an enormous impact on the children of Mapapa village. I still, however, don't know if we will make a lasting imprint on the larger community. Our work is creating new inroads, but at times I wonder if it is enough. I am not sure I will see all the deep cultural shifts that we are fighting for within my lifetime. The customs, beliefs, and practices in the villages of Zambia are much deeper and more entrenched in society than even

I—a native Zambian—realized. Social change is possible, but it may take a lifetime. The seeds that are now planted within the children are healthy, yet however strong, these seeds still need tending. They need water, sunshine, and rich soil. This is the mission of Footprints of Hope. We shall continue to both plant and nurture the seeds of our future.

I am proud of my journey. I am proud of the fact that Footprints of Hope was started by a single woman. I was alone with my thoughts and dreams. It took everything I had to take that first step, saying to myself, I will let go of everything else and chase this one dream. Each of us, regardless of our race, gender, or background, can make an incredible difference. We must simply have faith in ourselves and let kindness lead our way.

Dora Moono Nyambe

Chapter 1

"Yes." I nodded. "I need three hypodermic needles..."

The pharmacist looked back at me questioningly and I repeated myself, even more unsure than the first time. "Dora mentioned you would know which ones I need." "Oh, okay, yes these should work. You just need them for a blood test?" "Yes, for an HIV test, I believe."

I slid a worn ten-kwacha note across the glass counter and with a pained smile turned to leave. I ducked out of the doorway, having learned by now that short Zambian doorways tended to clip the top of my head, and scanned the street for the silver Toyota Prado. As I walked toward the car my nostrils filled with a mix of burning garbage, earthy vegetables, and live chickens being sold at the nearby market.

Masansa is an unremarkable rural town in the northern reaches of the Central Province of Zambia. It lies just two hours from the border of the Democratic Republic of Congo and about seven hours from Zambia's capital, Lusaka. It's an area that people—both foreign tourists and Zambians from other regions—simply don't visit. The roads are poor and there is not much to see aside from farmlands and the occasional reservoir. The town itself consists of one main intersection, a market, a gas station, agriculture shops, "Chinese goods" shops, a squat police station, a dozen or so tiny bars, and the Masansa Mini Hospital.

It was March of 2022 and I was living in Zambia, conducting ecotourism research as a Fulbright scholar. Just three months earlier, I had left my job as a management consultant in New York City and moved to Zambia to explore its varied landscapes, diverse culture, and abundant wildlife.

As I climbed into the car, Dora looked over to me with a forced yet characteristically sincere smile and said, "Not all days are this dark, I promise." She pulled the car away from the open gutter that flanked the side of the road and headed back to the Mini Hospital.

Dora wore a white blouse and dark pants. Her hair was pulled back in neatly braided rows and held together with a single hair tie. She was twenty-nine—a fact that was hard to decipher. Her physical appearance and upbeat energy could convince anyone that she was much younger, yet this youthful image was offset by the group of twelve children who called her Mommy. Everyone who meets Dora has a moment when they pause and try to make sense of her youth, her brood of children, and the many extraordinary things that happened to connect them.

The Masansa Mini hospital is made up of two long buildings and two small auxiliary US AID tents that stand in the background. The buildings are short, single-story cinder block rectangles sitting just a few yards apart and connected by a green metal awning. A two-room office building sits about ten meters behind the main structure, creating a square yard. Earlier that day, the Prado slowed to a crawl as we turned down the road to the hospital. The roads were so rutted near the entrance that I wondered to myself how anything smaller than a large 4x4 could pull in. Dora pulled the car into this grassy area, which was more mud than grass thanks to the rainy season, and parked. A lone Zambian flag languished from a skinny flagpole and people milled about. Across the muddy courtyard stood a line of pregnant women. It was a typical early morning with the heat beginning to rise and a perfectly clear sky.

I stepped out of the car, shadowing Dora as we approached a

young girl and her mother. Dora greeted them both in Bemba, a language I had first encountered upon traveling to this part of Zambia days earlier. As such, I only understood "Mwashibukeni," which means "Good morning." There are currently seventy-three recognized tribes and thirty distinct languages spoken throughout Zambia. Most Zambians speak at least two, if not three or more languages. English remains the national language and is widely spoken, though in varying degrees of fluency. Fortunately for me, Dora spoke English, Nyanja, and Bemba fluently.

Dora turned to me and said, "We will need to wait with her until we can get the necessary tests. Hopefully it isn't long." We proceeded through the courtyard, toward one of the small office buildings opposite the long hospital block. The four of us took seats on a wooden bench beneath the building's metal awning, escaping the heat while we waited. After a few minutes, someone stopped to speak with Dora. She stood and stepped away from the awning and into the sun. In quiet voices, Dora and the man spoke briefly before she turned to me and motioned to the car. The man was likely a physician or nurse; however, the lack of name tags or official uniforms made it hard to tell who was who. "We will need to buy hypodermic needles and rubber gloves to get the blood samples for the HIV and syphilis tests," she said.

The Zambian government provides free primary care services to all its citizens; however, the quality and accessibility of this care is highly varied. In the tiny village of Mapapa, where Dora's school is located, almost no one owns a vehicle. This meant that the trek to the hospital in Masansa could be an all-day affair. Hearing the doctor tell Dora she would need to fetch supplies was a jolt. I was shocked that the needles and other basic healthcare supplies weren't provided at the hospital. This was the first time I had witnessed a "bring your own supplies" healthcare system. But to Dora, having to buy these needles wasn't odd at all. I wondered if the line of pregnant women awaiting treatment would also be instructed to purchase their own medical supplies. The lack of basic resources at the hospital worried me deeply.

Dora turned right, pulling away from the hospital, and headed back into Masansa. Pulling up to the pharmacy, she parked the car. I offered to go in so she could keep the car running on the street. "I know Alfred really well," she said. "He's a friend of mine and the chemist here. If there's any trouble, just mention it's for me. He will know what to do." I nodded and ducked out of the car, jumping to clear the wide gutter and land on the sand median between the shops and the road. This is how I found myself buying hypodermic needles in a remote village.

That morning, I had woken up at Footprints of Hope, the boarding school and child welfare refuge Dora created in a tiny village about forty-five minutes west of Masansa. Dora asked me to be ready at 8:30, and I met her in front of her unpainted cinder block house. When I arrived, she was accompanied by a young girl. I greeted them both with a smile and was told the young girl's name was Nandi.

I had met many of the children when I first arrived at the school the night before. Nandi was nowhere near the youngest, yet this morning she looked smaller and more vulnerable than the others. She had dark brown eyes and I could barely make out her pupils. Her braided hair grazed the tops of her shoulders, and her body language looked as though she was trying to sink into the sand we stood on.

"How are you?" I asked.

She replied, stuttering her pre-rehearsed English line, "I-I-I am well and how are you?"

"I'm doing well, thank you."

Dora smiled broadly as she told me we would be going to the hospital and running a few errands. "I hope you don't mind. Hopefully it will give you an idea of what a normal day for me is like." I told her I was happy to join her and hopefully be of some use. Dora's smile never left her face as we got into the Prado with the windows rolled down and the sun just above the car's windshield. We headed east from the school toward the hospital in Masansa, a town I had yet to see.

Upon first arrival at the hospital, I felt out of place. Quickly scanning my surroundings, I'd spotted just three other men within the hospital compound. Dora motioned to a bench where we all sat and waited for assistance. Shortly after sitting down, we would make our excursion for needles and gloves before returning to the hospital. It was then that I began to comprehend the enormity of Dora's responsibility to the little girl seated beside me.

With the sun climbing increasingly high in the cloudless sky, the heat became oppressive. My stomach began to churn and I got up to search for a bathroom. The twelve guavas I had consumed the day before had come back with a vengeance. I followed the long gray rectangular building and turned to go behind it. The metal awning I walked under created a distinct tapping sound as the metal sheets expanded in the heat of the day. My stomach increasingly reminded me of the urgency of my situation. As I turned the corner, I nearly collided with the line of pregnant women and new mothers. It was clear they had been waiting all morning to see a doctor. I tried my best to shrink in size as I passed by. As a 6 foot 4 Caucasian male, my efforts to blend in were useless. Still, I felt the need to somehow reduce myself, to be less conspicuous. I caught a nurse's eye and asked for directions to the toilet. She pointed behind the building and I quickly turned and picked up speed. The only bathroom was a lone cinder block room with a rectangular hole cut in the center of the concrete floor. A small window ventilated the room, the roof above me seeming to work as an oven in the morning heat. Excrement was splattered around the proverbial drop zone. I squatted and flies began to incessantly dive bomb my face as I contorted and tried to relieve myself.

At this point, I'd been living in Zambia for three months and cursed myself for getting sick on this of all days. The reason for our visit to the hospital and the look on Nandi's face made my guava-induced sickness feel like a rude affront. Although the others didn't necessarily see it this way, I was embarrassed by my pale face and inherent weakness against the previous day's guava feast. My goal was to fit in and possibly be of some help, and instead I was becoming another person to care for.

I returned to the bench and found Dora and Nandi gone. Feeling slightly relieved (I felt my presence left others uncomfortable), I once again sat down and waited. Fifteen minutes later, Dora reappeared, walking across the courtyard from the hospital block toward me. "Could you possibly go and get Nandi a snack and something to drink?" she asked.

Eager to be useful, I drove the Prado to the main intersection in search of the nearest shop. Spotting a cinder block building with the words "General Dealer" hand painted across the top, I pulled the car to the side and entered. The store was dark with one light hanging behind the clerk's head. Dust swirled around the room and rested on each item, thinly veiling everything in sight. I bought four guavas, a Strawberry Milkit, and some biscuits. When I returned to the hospital I found Dora, Nandi, and Nandi's mother sitting on the bench waiting for some final paperwork. I handed the bag to Dora, who thanked me, and we all sat in silence while Nandi began to snack. Thirty minutes later, the three women went into the office; I waited outside.

Dora, visibly more tired than earlier, kept a positive and lighthearted tone. She looked across at me and spoke in swift clipped English. "We are going to the police station to file a report and then we will be done for the time being. This shouldn't take long." I quickly surmised that Nandi's mother would have no chance to understand our conversations if we spoke at anything beyond a slow pace. Even then I wondered how much English comprehension she had, given that she had spent her whole life living in a village that operated completely outside of the national language.

The Masansa police station is a one-story cinder block building about the size of a standard one-car garage. The rectangular station is painted white but has been stained brown by the dust constantly pelting it. The only indication of the building's purpose is the blue badge painted on the side of the station. We pulled the car into the yard where a few people loitered. One of them stepped out of a clearly broken-down car and followed us in. He too worked at the station but was avoiding the midafternoon heat in the building.

A plain-clothed female police officer greeted us warmly. I stood a few paces back as Dora spoke to her. It was clear they knew each other well, even seemed to be old friends. The officer seemed eager to help in whatever way possible. She shook my hand, introduced herself as Harriet, and led us into a tiny office. Quickly realizing the lack of space and seating, I excused myself and sat near the entrance of the station on a thin bench. A few minutes later, the three exited and Harriet thanked me for coming to Masansa. Dora explained that Harriet had been an enormous help in getting many children protection and prosecuting people who hurt them. I smiled at her, trying to convey some sort of appreciation for the difficult undertaking she had chosen as a career.

Dora and I waited in the car for Nandi to say goodbye to her mother. Dora explained that Nandi had been continually raped by her stepfather while under her mother's care. "We had her tested for STDs today and we know that she has contracted genital warts, syphilis, and possibly HIV," Dora said. "She's been through so much, and I honestly think her mother knew the whole time but never stepped in to stop it. The culture here enables men to do this because women are seen as bad wives if they override their husbands or leave. Nandi's body is a wreck right now. She is in so much pain."

Although I wasn't completely naive to the abuse Nandi suffered, at that point I had not known all the details of her situation. For the first time that day, Dora shared a moment of vulnerability. It was her way of unveiling how personally she took what was going on in this young girl's life. Nandi was ten years old. Until today, this child had not had a single person advocating for her. Now Dora had stepped up. This young girl now had someone on her side, someone looking out for her, and with that her life would be changed forever. Dora continued, explaining the physical damage to the girl's body, the smell she emitted, and her undoubted psychological scars. I had known of Dora for quite some time and was taken by her mission to educate and feed those in this rural and impoverished area. But it wasn't until this moment that I began to comprehend the gravity of the battle she was fighting, a burden she shouldered largely outside the public eye. What stuck with me the most that day was Dora's optimism, the outward positivity she showed despite such a burden.

Nandi looked relieved as she opened the Prado's side door

and climbed in. We made one last stop at the market on our way home. Dora said, "Let me just grab one quick thing. I'll be right back. You two stay here."

I turned back toward Nandi, assuming she felt uncomfortable being left alone with a relative stranger, and said, "I'm hungry, would you like a fritter?"

She smiled and nodded shyly.

"Okay, let's get some!" I rolled down the window and motioned to a woman across the street who was selling fried dough out of a plastic container. I bought six for the price of 35 cents and then the two of us sat and snacked quietly. I thought about the strength Dora had shown in bringing this girl into her life. Dora was only five years my senior and was working to dramatically change lives. What that vision was exactly was still becoming clear to me. There was much more to this woman than a GoFundMe page and successful online presence. Before I had time to think much more, Dora opened the car door and we were once again heading back toward Footprints of Hope—the small oasis erected to educate, feed, and protect children.

Footprints of Hope is not just a free rural boarding school but rather a full-blown development project. Two years earlier, Dora had moved to the remote village of Mapapa with two of her adopted children. They built a mud hut to live in, and

Dora began teaching underneath a tree. Without institutional support and nothing but her meager savings, Dora's development mission began. Prior to this, she had spent years working for mission organizations, but she wanted to break away and run an organization based on her vision. Despite the many risks, she was able to begin by harnessing the power of social media. Dora shared her journey via social media, garnering over 3.8 million followers whom she enlisted to help fund her goals. Her impact as an education and girls' rights advocate has reached millions of people around the world. Dora's optimistic personality and unrelenting efforts have connected more effectively with donors than many other highly funded organizations and development groups. In turn, her school that was born under a tree now has eighty students living full time on campus and another hundred day students. Every student receives three meals and two snacks and spends five days a week in classes. Bemba, the local language, is strictly forbidden on campus, and all conversations, no matter how much the students struggle, are held in English. Although this sounds harsh, the truth is that by learning to read, write, and speak in English, which is Zambia's national language, the children's chances of escaping poverty improve exponentially.

Dora was initially guarded with me, and the more I came to appreciate why, the better I began to understand her. Often soft and caring with the children, Dora also took charge and was a disciplinarian. The school looked to her alone for strength during difficult times. Dora had worked with some of the most vulnerable people on earth and experienced trauma of her own. The mission she had taken up as her life work, however, offered little assurance in regard to stability. Funding for the school is completely reliant on both social media and the global perception of one person—Dora. Her success, while unprecedented, also means she has few others to turn to for advice or assurances. Footprints of Hope, Dora's NGO, is trying to fund grassroots development through social media.

Chapter 2

In January of 2022, I passed through security in Chicago's O'Hare International airport. I could physically feel the tightness in my head improving as I walked toward the gate. Due to the COVID-19 pandemic there were times I thought my move to Zambia and subsequent research were in jeopardy of being canceled. I was now cleared for a journey across 13,000 kilometers to my new home, Zambia. It was a country I had never visited, only studied and written about.

Zambia is a landlocked nation in Southern Africa that shares borders with eight countries: Angola, Tanzania, Zimbabwe, Namibia, The Democratic Republic of Congo, Mozambique, Malawi, and Botswana. Recently, the Zambian president adopted the phrase "land linked,"[1] which is perhaps a creative way to say that everything costs 25 to 50 percent more due to transport, tariffs, and import taxes. It is home to just over twenty million people. Over 99 percent of the population is considered to be black Africans, with the less than 1 percent of non-black Zambians living mostly in the urban areas.[2] There are seventy-two distinct ethnic groups, each of which has its own language.[3] The country is largely supported by two industries: copper mining and agriculture. Geographically impressive, Zambia has varied landscapes and ecosystems. It has a landmass twice the size of Germany and is slightly larger than the US state of Texas. My interest in Zambia stemmed largely from its hugely diverse population and massive swaths of federally protected lands. Among this land is the nation's most famous attraction, Victoria Falls, which is the world's largest waterfall. There are twenty national parks and thirty-four game management areas. Some are considered among the top game parks in the world whereas others remain largely undeveloped. I was particularly interested in one of the least developed national parks, Sioma Ngwezi. I had come to Zam-

---

[1] "Zambia Is Land Linked State - President Hichilema," LusakaTimes.com, November 16, 2021

[2] "World Population Prospects 2022". *population.un.org*. United Nations Department of Economic and Social Affairs, Population Division

[3] "Zambian People" Zambiantoursim.com | Tribes in Zambia

bia to do research on the economic effects of ecotourism on communities within Sioma Ngwezi National Park.

Ecotourism provides a unique opportunity for local communities to make economic strides in development while conserving their national parks. A study on the economic impact of ecotourism within Sioma Ngwezi National Park had yet to be completed. Sioma Ngwezi was of particular interest to me due to its lack of infrastructure. Understanding the perceived benefits gained from ecotourism as a development model is essential for the analysis of its shortcomings. The goal remains to provide proper benefit-sharing principles stemming from ecotourism among tourist operators, federal organizations, local communities, and conservation groups. When all parties involved benefit from tourism, challenges such as wildlife degradation, poaching, and illegal logging will continue to decline. As a researcher, the chance to run my own project, work with remote community leaders, collect data, and provide valuable information drew me to Zambia.

Just days prior to arriving in Zambia, I had set up a TikTok account to share updates on my research and life. I wanted to learn about the different ethnic groups and hopefully share some of that knowledge with others. As a Fulbright researcher, I had a responsibility to create cross-cultural ties between nations. Social media was a way to share experiences with a broad group of Zambians as well as Americans. At the time, I had no idea how significant my social media interactions would prove to be.

I first saw Dora on TikTok when I arrived in Zambia. My TikTok account "@explorewithjoe" was opened in January of 2022 and began with updates on my research and move to Zambia. A few of my first videos while in Zambia went viral, or at least for me, 50,000 to 150,000 views felt viral. While scrolling through the comments on a video captioned "Why I had moved to Zambia" I saw a woman named Dora Moono Nyambe tagged several times. In one of the tagged comments she had replied, "I'd love to have you share this in a lesson format to my students." Next to her name was a blue check mark signifying she was verified, which in the digital world states your relative importance and often celebrity status. Intrigued, I clicked on her profile.

Just six weeks later, in February, I was walking side by side with Dora and the other teachers at her boarding school in Mapapa village. Leading up to this visit, Dora had messaged me via Tiktok and we began to talk both about her work and my interest in visiting her and learning more. While driving to the remote village, I anticipated a short one- to two-day visit. My expectations for the visit were grounded mainly in the idea of meeting an interesting person. Perhaps I would get the chance to read with some students and play some fun games. Dora had told me there would be room for me to stay; nonetheless, I brought a tent and my camping stove, unsure of what to expect. Prior to traveling to the school, I told a fellow researcher that I would likely be gone one, maximum two nights. The last thing I wanted to do was overstay my welcome.

Midmorning on my second day at the school, I trailed the five female teachers toward Kamanda. Zambia's rainy season, November to March, was coming to an end and the large pools of water that had accumulated were beginning to dry. As the water cleared, a vibrant stretch of red earth, pockmarked by massive divots made by industrial vehicles, once again became usable as a main road. Despite walking, I was still struck by the road conditions, which even on foot were a challenge to navigate.

The wide metal gate swung to a close behind our group, the metal clanging against the bright polka-dot-colored cement walls holding it upright on either side. Our group consisted of Dora, four other female teachers, and me. Turning west away from the gate, we set out down the dirt road on foot. Enormous blue gum trees lined the road on the right, framing the farmland behind them. To the left there was nothing but virgin bush. The stark contrast of the industrial farmland and the bushland was particularly jarring. As we slowly paraded down the road, we passed the occasional mud and straw hut, occupied by an entire family, and the smell of wood-burning fires wafted over as families prepared their first meal of the day. Across the road the slight vibrations of irrigation systems could be heard in the distance. Food was being grown in abundance, using clean water ten yards from people whose greatest challenge was food insecurity and securing potable water for themselves.

Teacher Dora, as she is referred to by colleagues and parents alike, had decided to take us on a walk through the village. It was her way of reinforcing the remaining challenges while visiting with the community she served. She excitedly told us, "This is Kamanda, where many of our students come from and is our neighboring village. For those of you who just joined our school, I'm excited for you to meet some of the community members and see our work here."

Turning off the main road, Dora led us down a narrow dirt path that was lined on either side by tall elephant grass. The rains had created a lush world of green that seemed to swallow anyone up if they got farther than a few paces ahead. It was hot, but there were few mosquitos or other insects that required swatting, making the morning stroll pleasant. As we followed her in silence, Dora would often pause, seemingly to breathe in each aspect of our walk as we approached the village. The farther we ventured from the main road, the more she seemed to relax. Kamanda has a population of only a few hundred and is connected by narrow dirt paths; there are no official roads or even obvious landmarks to direct someone unfamiliar with the area.

We approached a small clearing where three young children, two girls and a boy, stared blankly at us. The two girls wore simple cotton dresses stained from their dinner the night before and covered in dust. The young boy looked similarly dirty in his pants and t-shirt marked with dozens of small holes. The earth we stood on consisted mainly of sand, and staying "clean" as a child was next to impossible as dust was kicked up by the slightest movement. The teachers began to greet the two youngest girls in Bemba and the older boy in English.

Dora turned back to me and said, "This is where Teacher Victor lives. It's his parents' home and these are his nieces and nephews." The clearing contained three modest buildings: an open straw hut for storage and shade, a cooking hut with low mud walls and a large gap at the top for ventilation, and a small mud home with a thatched roof. A lone pit latrine stood in the far corner of the property, and yellow water jugs waited by the doorway of the house to be filled. The group sat down on two wooden benches, and I found a log to sit on, directly opposite Teacher Thandiwe.

Thandiwe is the "head teacher" and the second person I met the day I arrived at the school. She has a big smile and laughs with her whole body when she cracks jokes and pokes fun at her peers. Humor is Thandiwe's way of bringing the larger group together. The faculty is varied in their backgrounds, and I found it hard to communicate with many of them beyond basic conversations. Laughing at and with one another, sometimes despite not fully understanding a joke, truly did create inroads to each other for the entire group. She and another teacher were both pregnant and about four months away from being new mothers. Only a few years my senior, Thandiwe seemed a lifetime older as she prepared to start a new family. Three large chickens dashed behind me and I turned, somewhat startled. Thandiwe looked at me with raised eyebrows, as if to say, Watch out, they are man-eaters! and we both began to laugh. As our laughter died down, Teacher Victor exited the modest thatched roof home and approached us. His hands clasped in front of him about chest high, he greeted each of us and welcomed us to his home.

Teacher Victor has a strong and stoic presence. Later I would learn his family refers to him as "the soldier" and are always somewhat wary of his quiet and reserved nature. I found this to be an accurate portrayal of his physical presence and body language. When I first met Victor, it appeared as if he had just walked out of a midtown Manhattan office building. When I observed him in class, he was dressed in a pressed button-down shirt and khaki pants, sporting suede Chelsea boots. Now, seeing him in a t-shirt and shorts at his parents' home, I was struck by the contrast. He is tall and has an impressive build, yet with children he seemed to shrink and become as tender as a fellow student. At the time Teacher Victor was the only male teacher; he showed a great deal of respect for Dora and Teacher Thandiwe. Even with my limited cultural knowledge, I knew having female leaders, especially in a rural area, was rare. Dora asked Teacher Victor to fetch some water for the two pregnant women and he obliged, ducking into the house. Meanwhile Dora mobilized the group. "Let's make a TikTok with Teacher Joe, using our favorite dance song, 'My Bestie.'" Laughing, I hopped up and joined the group as Dora positioned her phone on a wooden chair and then faced us. "Okay, so I'll start the music and everyone needs to start dancing in place then we go into the choreographed dance. Let's do a practice one!"

Watching Dora direct the small production was a behind the scenes look at how she had become a social media sensation. Her energy and body language conveyed how much she enjoyed the whole production. She would point to us as if to say "Get into the spirit," making each person laugh as she did so. If the video was never posted, viewed, or liked, it seemed as if she wouldn't care; the dancing and laughter was her end goal.

The group of teachers now accompanied by Teacher Victor once more began to walk deeper into Kamanda. Ahead was a concrete platform with a metal pump protruding from the center. Dora turned back towards me and motioned ahead to the small monument, 'This is one of the five boreholes I installed with money that was generated from the GoFundMe. Technically they are all on our land, but that's just because I wanted to keep ownership of them so that no one in the village tries to stop others from using them for free." I nodded as another teacher began to rock the metal handle up and down to pump water. I watched intently as the group filled their bottles and began to drink.

Zambia is a country filled with fresh water. It's home to the mighty Zambezi, the fourth largest river in the world. After gaining independence from the British, the nation would derive its name from this iconic river that hugs its western border. The country is also host to several massive lakes, such as Mweru, Tanganyika, and Bangweulu. In the southwestern corner of the country is the world's largest man-made lake by volume, damming the Zambezi as it flows toward the Indian Ocean. As a nation, Zambians have some of the most abundant freshwater resources of any country in sub-Saharan Africa.

Despite this abundance, all water is not created equal. It was one of the first and most important lessons Dora taught me that day. "It's really frustrating when I hear people, mainly Africans actually, who joke about, oh Africa has no water and then they switch the camera to reveal a lake or a river. The point of these videos is to highlight the lack of knowledge foreigners have about Africa and to mock stereotypes. I get why some people think it's funny, however this can actually be very harmful. It's because these videos also don't tell the whole story. The truth is not all water is drinkable. When I moved here, we were getting water from an open pit well just like all of the other villagers. There were frogs living in the well and small animals would often fall in and drown. It was our only water source and if the rains didn't come our supply was threatened. Potable water and freshwater are not the same. When people say that Zambia has plenty of water, they are not telling you the whole truth. It's about access to clean drinkable water."

Dora was right. Over 70 percent of rural people in Zambia don't have access to proper sanitation, and about 50 percent don't have access to clean drinking water.[4] These statistics are likely underestimating the true magnitude of the issue,

---

[4] Assessing the Affordability of Water, Sanitation and Hygiene: Zambia Country Case Study | UNICEF & World Health Organization - Zachary Burt, Akmal Abdurazakov & Guy Hutton

as polling and field screening in Zambia have limited scope. I was standing next to a borehole that, if taken care of properly, should provide clean drinking water for generations of families. The woman standing in front of me, filling her water bottle, had moved to a remote village in the bush and began a development campaign with no institutional support or funding. Being able to drink clean potable water from a well that hadn't existed just a few months earlier was a testament to her incredible progress.

As we walked, Dora kept up a constant commentary. She spoke in a conversational tone, without the need to use a "teacher voice" to distinguish her as the teacher and the rest of us as students. Everything we passed had a story and everything was a lesson on how the lives of the locals had been and could continue to be improved. Like the village students she ate in the school's dining hall, and now it was as though she was feeding us. She was offering sustenance throughout the hike in the form of thought and lessons learned throughout the past years. She is a natural storyteller and has a knack of making you want to listen longer and learn more.

"Joshua!" Dora cried out with a smile as a young boy about the age of four came careening down the dirt path. He was barefoot and had a wide smile. His little laugh made everyone around him smile. He stopped abruptly in front of us and eyed me carefully. Though we had met a few days prior, he was skeptical about seeing me in his village. Teacher Dora, always the educator, asked Joshua a few questions in English, and after a pause he acquiesced and everyone rewarded him with praise.

Two older women greeted the group in Bemba as we crossed through their yard. Dora responded, using their names and asking how they were. As we continued to walk past numerous households, villagers seemed to materialize to greet the teachers, specifically Dora. Except for a few staff members, every person at the school came from the surrounding area. This meant apart from Dora, I was the only one not born within ten to fifteen miles of our location. To Dora, these people seemed to be friends and people she cared about. From their perspective, Dora was a community leader and somewhat of an alien. A single mother who had somehow brought development and education to a poor area, despite being desperately poor herself.

The path began to meander away from the congregation of homes and out toward scraggly fields of planted crops. The villagers rely mainly on subsistence farming, apart from a few who own small shops in the neighboring village or work for one of the large farm blocks across from Footprints of Hope. Despite a physically demanding life and living in what many would describe as abject poverty, the people seemed to be happy. This appearance of general satisfaction was something I resisted at first. I was afraid of being another foreigner viewing the village through a one-way mirror as an "idyllic poor village," yet another trope in the Western playbook. I could see, however, that happiness can exist in places where misery is perceived as common. A marriage or a new baby is still cause for celebration, even if it doesn't mean that illness, hunger, sexual abuse, and all that underdevelopment entails isn't still present. To many of the villagers I met, this duality of happiness and poverty was not something that was dwelled on; it was simply how things were.

Dora understands this nuance of life more than anyone. She is a complex person herself who by millions over the internet is seen through a single lens: "the village TikToker" and "Saint Dora." Walking through the village, my narrow perception of what village life was began to crumble. Once more we found ourselves approaching a concrete circle with a gleaming metal water pump. Ringed by a small cluster of trees, we rested at the borehole. As the sun reached its apex directly above us, we relaxed in the shade of the trees. Dora glanced at me and I followed her to the back of the clearing where she pointed to the open field beyond the trees. "You see those power lines out in the distance?" I looked back at her and nodded. "We own all the land from the road going all the way back to those power lines. Currently we have another two classrooms that need to be built at the primary school, but after that I need to build a secondary school. I'm going to put it right back there." She gazed through the trees onto the open field with its waves of elephant grass that looked like an ocean of green.

"How much will that cost?" Always a pragmatist, my mind immediately jumped to all the potential roadblocks. Instead of seeing my question as prying or even a detractor, Dora replied sweetly, "A lot!" She laughed. "As much as I can get!" This response also made me laugh. I admired her confidence. To Dora, a secondary school wasn't the next stage in her plan, it was something that needed to have happened yesterday. Her mind ruminated on where her precious sixth grade class would go if she did not build them a school.

Urgency isn't a marketing tool used to motivate donors from across the world. Ten, twenty, thirty years ago it was urgent that these people get an education, access to clean water, and end food scarcity among children. To say it was now overdue would be an understatement. Dora is not a voice for these children. She doesn't write reports on the need to educate children; she just invites them into the classroom. She doesn't go to conferences to denounce the atrocity of child marriages; she marches into tiny village police stations and demands it is stopped. Her work isn't graphed, charted, or peer reviewed. She just gets things done. Much of Dora's story is hidden within the children she helps. She is an "actionist" not an activist. She isn't angry or pointing fingers; rather, she is determined to change the standard of what is seen as acceptable. The government, either incapable or incompetent, makes little difference to her and the villagers. If children lack education, healthcare, proper nutrition, and are being forced into early marriages, it is only going to change through radical action. Despite what many NGOs try to ignore, this change is often closely intertwined with culture and as such, must be rooted out by an insider. Culturally, Dora is shaking up what is seen as acceptable and that angers many. Change is rarely popular even among those whom it could benefit the most. However, even those she upsets also hope her vision will become a reality.

My view of Footprints of Hope was beginning to shift. As someone who had watched Dora's videos and read about her online, the impression I had arrived with was based simply on the premise that Dora was a teacher and ran a rural school. However, the school and Dora herself are far more complex than the face value representation seen on the internet. Footprints of Hope is a large-scale community development effort, one that likely will take a lifetime. As for Dora, she had spent years prior to moving to Mapapa working with mission organizations building the skills to pursue such an endeavor. She feels deeply compelled to educate and protect children. Dora's involvement in the community is in no way limited to just providing education and wells. It is far greater.

As we looked out at that field, I couldn't ignore the power inside the woman standing beside me. When Dora moved to the village in 2019, the school she would eventually go on to build was nothing more than a dream. She arrived with her two adopted daughters and built a simple one-room mud hut complete with a straw roof. It was a modest but absolute commitment, regardless of the outcome. Since then, life had been uncertain, even treacherous for Dora who as a single mother was attempting to launch an underfunded school miles from the nearest settlement. Her first home would begin to disintegrate due to a termite infestation, and her second, more "stable" house would partially collapse. Unfortunately, Dora's first classroom didn't fare well either. The mud and straw building was swallowed up by a bush fire, forcing her to start from scratch once again. I watched this journey retroactively, whereas millions of others watched it unfold in real time on TikTok.

Back at the school, Dora and the teaching staff were showered with "Hellos," waves, and compliments. "You look very nice, Teacher." These children, with their three or four English compliments, would make anyone feel like a rockstar. Within the school property's barbed wire perimeter fence, a curved road leads students and staff through campus. We first passed the playground, which provides an open field for sports, mainly football and handball. Behind the playground is the main classroom block, which at the time had eight classrooms and the large rectangular dining hall. The school still lacked any power. Continuous strings of smoke could be seen rising from various points around the school where fires were being used for cooking and heating water for bathing. As the road curves to the left, the "beginners' classroom," which serves the youngest members of the school, stands opposite the staff housing which is walled off by a thatched fence. Finally, the gendered dormitories lie at opposite ends of the property separated by a wide distance of over eighty meters. The last few buildings at the very back of the property are Dora's home and a guest house occupied by the head teacher, Thandiwe. As the teaching staff dispersed to take care of various activities, Aunties and Uncles milled about. These are staff members tasked with everything from security and maintenance to childcare and cleaning. They are referred to by name, prefaced by Auntie or Uncle, similar to how many would use Mr. and Mrs.

As Dora approached her house, I watched as four of her girls came running out to greet her. They showered her with their standard English compliments and then her smallest daughter, only three and whose head seemed comically too large for her body, came trotting behind them. Five children constituted a large family; however, this was less than half of the Nyambe brood at the time. The other six were in various parts of the country; three were in boarding school and the other three were over eighteen. The eldest three were largely out of Dora's direct care, yet never far from her mind. The final member was Nandi, who since arriving at the school had been staying with Dora. Adoption in Zambia is not overly common, and I would come to learn the legal system in no way assisted Dora in her efforts to provide for her children.

Each part of Dora's life raised questions about who she was and the journey she had undertaken. Prior to leaving the school after my first visit in February, I sat down with Dora to film a short interview with the camera and tripod I always travel with. The night before, she knocked on my door and asked to come in. We sat at the kitchen table and under the intensely bright solar LED light ran through the questions I planned to ask. For the first time I heard directly from Dora as to how she views her past and the way it has brought her to the current moment. With every step I took toward possibly understanding this person, who she was seemed to become less clear. Dora wasn't facing traditional challenges that could be overcome in a matter of years. Many of the greatest impediments to her vision for the children of Mapapa would be a continuing struggle until long-term cultural changes can take root. As we finished up our discussion, I had one unscripted question: "Why are you doing all of this? Is it really just to help people?"

"I saw a need," she responded without pausing. "That's the reason I started all of this."

On my final day of that first week, Dora and I filmed the interview. Thinking that a recorded interview could be of use to her, perhaps for outreach to donors, I offered to film and edit the video. She agreed, thinking it could be an easy piece of content to share on YouTube, a platform she used sporadically. That morning we recorded a fifteen-minute interview. I asked about her NGO, her childhood, and the work she had done internationally. After so many great conversations that dove deeper into her past and aspirations for the future, we both were optimistic that the interview could help propel her important work.

The rest of the afternoon I spent time taking photos of every child at the school. I planned to create composite photos of each class as a gift to the students and staff for hosting me. My short visit had nearly come to an end. I was headed back to my research area in the Western Province of Zambia, a sixteen-hour drive to the southwestern part of the country. My visit to the school had been born completely out of intrigue about meeting Dora. As a foreign researcher I saw my job as two-fold. First, to provide valuable data and insight into my research topic. Second, and equally important to me during my time in Zambia, was to learn from others and better understand the experiences of others.

After just a week, I had forged friendships with many of the staff members and was calling students by their names. Leaving the following morning, I felt as though I had witnessed something very special. Footprints of Hope is a place that no TikTok or YouTube video could accurately capture. At that moment, I thought it would be a memory, a place and group of people I alone would cherish.

The drive from Mkushi to Sioma Ngwezi is a grueling slog. Arriving home late in the evening, I was exhausted but filled with excitement to create my gift for the students and edit Dora's interview. I woke the next morning eager to get started on what I was sure could be a compelling piece of content. I reviewed the raw footage once. And then again. All the magic and inspiration I had felt and witnessed was nowhere. Dora had provided insightful answers about her time at the school, working in India, and her vision for Footprints of Hope. Yet, when I reviewed the tape, it was lacking the spirit of what had moved me so greatly while at the school. Somehow the complexity and grit of what was being accomplished was missing. Footprints of Hope and Dora Moono Nyambe's journey were anything but linear, but together we had portrayed them both as just that. I texted Dora that she should wait to see the interview until I returned and that I would think of a better way to communicate her incredible story.

Six weeks later I was back at the school. Dora and I had spent a day running errands together; she had asked me to drive, and I was happy to do so. As I turned into the gate, Dora asked me, "Have you ever considered writing a book about all your travels?" I had ruminated for weeks on how to bring up the idea of writing about her and she had beaten me to it.

"How about I write a book about you instead? I've thought about it a lot and I'd be honored to help share your story in a meaningful way."

"Let me put on a business suit tonight and we can talk about it!"

I laughed and pulled up to her house. Our journey was about to begin.

Chapter 3

Dora bent slightly at the waist, bringing her face closer to Simon's as she greeted him. I smiled, watching through the large square windows of the dining hall, my head slightly cocked as I peered over the rebar that crosshatched the window and obstructed my view. Little Simon, as Dora lovingly refers to him, was one of her longtime students and a special case. Simon was nine years old, but I would have guessed his age to be closer to five or six. Even his hands and eyes seemed particularly small. While out in the village doing what most would call a welfare check, Dora met Simon. She had started these walks when she arrived as a way to become more integrated into the community and learn about the families. As an outsider, I saw this as a form of social work. Dora, however, would never concede to this, saying things like, "I was hearing about a problem and a potential student we could help. So I'd go see for myself." I would come to learn that Dora, like all of us, has an ego, but when it comes to how others see the school, she always works to downplay her own efforts.

At the time she met Simon he was only seven years old and a severely malnourished sick child. Malnutrition has plagued this area due to several reasons such as lack of family planning, subsistence farming creating a reliance on weather, alcoholism, and the overall lack of economic opportunity. The long and short of why children were not getting fed came down to poverty. Young children who are chronically malnourished are at a higher risk of developing liver enzyme imbalances that can permanently damage their health and in some cases are fatal.[5] When Dora first met Simon, his liver was not the first thing on her mind; his underdeveloped body and sickly nature were the most obvious and pressing matters.

The boys sitting in front of me eagerly spooned their morning sampo into their mouths. Zambian food is not widely available around the world and as such just about everything I tried in those first few months was a new experience. Sampo is a porridge consisting of maize, groundnuts, and peanut

---

[5] Starvation-induced Liver Enzyme Elevation after Initiation of Feeding | Intern Med. 2019 Mar 1, Nishioka H, Yoshizaki A, Imai Y, Higashibeppu N.

butter added for flavor. As the boys made faces at me across the wooden picnic table, students filed in and out of the dining hall. The loud clanking of their metal bowls being piled up reverberated off the cinder block structure. When asked how their breakfast tasted, they replied without fail in their rehearsed English, "Delicious, Teacher!" As the mountain of bowls began to rise, I got up to leave. Breathing carefully, I walked through the thin haze of dust kicked up from the students scurrying over the sand floor.

Mornings were always a flurry of excitement as happy students eagerly munched at whatever maize-inspired food was presented. Dora greeted me and I inquired about Simon's health. "Little Simon is one of our special cases. He looks so little but he's actually in fourth grade. He was severely malnourished and sick a lot over the past two years. We finally were able to get him looked at by a specialist and he has liver problems. For now he's healthy, but..." She trailed off as we both watched Simon scamper away.

In the first years of her life, Dora was also a sick child. She was born in June 1992 at a hospital in Kabwe, a city just a few hours south of our current location. Dora's mother, Rose Thazi, recalls rushing back to Zambia from a business trip in South Africa just nine days before her due date. She said, "My uncle advised me to drop whatever I was doing and come back to Zambia. Otherwise, Dora could have been born in South Africa or Zimbabwe and it would have been very difficult to bring her home." At the time, Rose was working as an independent importer. Buying consumer products on a small scale in South Africa, she would bring them back to Lusaka to sell them at a markup. "By then business was good," she recalled. "I used to deal mostly in ladies clothing and shoes. Then at some point, I switched to groceries and then finally to supplying hardware." Rose herself was born in 1955 in South Africa. Her stepfather who raised her was a Zambian and her mother a South African. Dora also had a split nationality. Her mother, despite living most of her life in Zambia, identified more closely with her South African heritage. Dora's father hailed from the Western Province of Zambia and was part of the Lozi tribe. He had never been a part of Dora's life and based on her assertion, only contributed his Lozi and Zambian lineage to Dora.

Dora spent her formative childhood years with her mother in a rental house in Lusaka's Mutendere neighborhood. The house consisted of two rooms and a living room, with an exposed metal roof overhead. The bathroom, a pit latrine, was located a few paces behind the house. When describing the bathroom Dora recalled, "There was a seat but my mom never allowed us to sit on it. It was made out of blocks [cinder block] so you had to squat." The house was close to the tarmac road, and running water was found at the tap just outside the front door. "It was a really good house, that first one I won't forget, mm hmm." Dora identifies her native tongue as English, but she also learned Nyanja at a very young age. "All the neighborhood kids and I would speak in English. We thought it was posh," she told me through a laugh. Rose's job required her to travel to neighboring African countries, which meant Dora was frequently left under the care of an Auntie her mother hired.

Rose often returned from these work trips with small toys for Dora, who subsequently shared them with all the neighborhood children. "She was very popular, you know. She had a lot of friends. When Dora had to wash dishes before going out to play, her friends would chip in so they could get to playing with her and her toys faster," Rose recalled with a laugh. Despite her playmates, Dora had a hard time keeping up physically. Unknown to her mother, Dora was born with an undiagnosed weak heart valve. Dora recalled how often she had to stop playing completely while running around with friends and just lie on the ground until she could regain her strength. Her health issues persisted but became less debilitating as she got older.

Rose enrolled Dora in private schooling at age five because the government schools didn't enroll children until they were six. This meant that throughout her schooling Dora was often the youngest in her class. Despite not being a straight A student, school was somewhere Dora felt safe. She struggled with dyslexia, a form of learning disability not widely recognized in Zambia at the time, which made reading and writing particularly difficult. Rather than developing a distaste for reading, the challenge intrigued Dora. Her mother encouraged her reading and Dora took pride in developing an extensive vocabulary. Nonetheless, the way others treated her dyslexia and the impact it had on her confidence is evident to this day. It is a vein of insecurity that Dora still carries traces of and willingly recognizes. "Constantly being told I was stupid throughout schooling definitely impacted me... Yes, there were a lot of negative voices," was the best way she could sum up how it felt as a young person working to overcome a misunderstood disability.

Rose consistently tried to improve their lives and encouraged those around her as well. "I've always trusted my neighbors and pushed them to understand the importance of excelling in life through education," she told me. Rose purchased a plot of land in a different part of Lusaka and began to build a home and a few small tenant houses. For a single mother with meager financial security, this was a bold move. "My mother was the only single mother in our first two neighborhoods, and she worked very hard," Dora said, thinking back to their time in Mutendere.

The two moved shortly after the completion of the first home. Despite her dyslexia and the challenges it brought, Dora enjoyed learning and was thankful to attend private schools, which offered better education than the government standard. It was clear to Dora that her mother prioritized her education, something she always highlighted when talking about this time in her life. When speaking with Rose, there was a clear disconnect between how the two perceived Dora's educational struggles and social acceptance. Dora herself described their relationship as "distant," telling me that "my mother was a very hard worker and did her best. She and I were not close emotionally and have never had that friendly relationship I saw others have with their parents." This lack of closeness with her own mother juxtaposed Dora's parenting style. With her own children, Dora is tender and affirmation is poured out generously.

When asked if she ever felt poor growing up, Dora remained silent for a second, thinking. "I've never gone hungry. We always had enough and I didn't even know what rich was! My mother and I seemed to always have everything we needed, but not more." As she said this, one of the older boys, Granson, stepped into view and timidly interrupted our conversation.

It was a sunny afternoon and the cat Dora had rescued was curled up on the couch between us. Bruno, the sleepy orange fluffball, looked up at the boy who explained he had brought guavas from his parents as a gift for Teacher Dora. She thanked him and he knelt, bowing his head as he handed over the fruit.

Dora most definitely didn't grow up with abundance; however, her childhood wasn't a tale of scarcity either. Talking with her, I understood that times were often harder than she wanted to admit. She was proud of the things she had been through, a pride I felt guarded some of the most difficult memories. As I watched Granson head back toward the dormitory, it was hard not to think that these children felt similarly while at the school. There was cake for the occasional party, toys were shared, but everyone always had plenty to eat and clothes on their backs. Yes, the clothes were secondhand and oftentimes "misgendered." I would see boys running around with "girlie" slogans printed across their chests and girls wearing "boys" winter jackets. Gender constructs were far from the thoughts of children who were happy to have clean, quality clothes. School was a safe place for these kids, a place of stability. Yes, they had their basic needs covered, and when Dora described "always having enough," I know she meant this.

On an early Tuesday morning in April, Dora and I climbed

into the silver Prado. Since my return to the school, the rains had ended and the roads were once again becoming navigable. No longer were there small lakes between the undulating dirt and sand roads that connected the various small villages and farm blocs throughout the Luano District. Not one to ask for favors, Dora preferred to ride as a passenger, and I was eager to be of some nominal use. Most of our days looked like this, running errands, community visits, and me watching as Dora administered to all sorts of issues surrounding the school. All the while, I sat next to her, scribbling away in a notebook and peppering her with questions. Somehow, she always made time for my queries, never accusing me when my language failed to put things in kind ways. As we pulled away from the Chinese import store in Masansa, I commented on how much a baby, the child of the woman running the store, had loved Dora. The woman was a friend of Dora's. At this point I had learned she was friends with just about everyone who owned a business. This was in part because she was an excellent customer. At the time, the school was providing three meals a day for about 150 people, which meant Footprints of Hope was purchasing food for 450 to 500 hot meals a day. Aside from food, Dora was buying medicine, building supplies, and everything under the sun for her development efforts. Dora paid in cash and was willing to place orders ahead of time. This made Dora a dream customer for the small merchants of Masansa. Although this meant she had good relations and friends who ran businesses, it also meant it was hard to decipher if they were real friends or just business acquaintances. Observing her in these first weeks, I often wondered how isolated she was socially.

But when Dora walked into the store, the little girl's eyes had lit up. Dora gingerly scooped her onto her hip. The little girl cooed while Dora ordered a few things from the girl's mother and the three of us made small talk. Navigating back to the school, we crawled past the enormous trash heap welcoming you to Masansa. It was a reminder that basic sanitation and government services are not a given in this part of the country. Somewhat absentmindedly as I navigated the potholes that threatened to swallow the Prado I asked, "When was the first time you really stuck your neck out and helped someone?"

"Did I tell you about the time I helped a pregnant woman at a bus station?" she asked.

As a twelve-year-old, Dora had been traveling alone in Lusaka to visit extended family who lived across the city. Arriving at the large central bus terminal, she headed over to the food court, taking a seat near the back. Dora was a streetsmart and confident young woman. The central bus station in Lusaka is overwhelmingly busy. Dozens of massive Greyhound buses pull in every ten to fifteen minutes, and hundreds of smaller white vans that act as both long and short forms of transportation speed about.

When I imagined her sitting there on a summer day avoiding the heat, it was hard not to be stressed on her behalf. This bus station was host to a large population of street children, drugs, and prostitution. Even as a grown man, I was more alert every time I passed through this part of the capital. It wasn't a place where I was overly worried about my safety, but rather more cognizant of the vast differences in my life and those around me. In 2010 when Dora was passing through this station, Lusaka was one of the fastest growing cities on the planet.

While waiting for a relative, Dora overheard a conversation between a restaurant owner and a very young pregnant woman. She was from Mongu, a city eight hours away in the Western Province. Her boyfriend had told her to come and retrieve some money in the capital from him. Upon her arrival, he had disappeared, and she was now stranded without money and far from her relatives. The girl appeared dirty and distressed. "I approached her and asked if I could talk with her. She was confused as to why I cared. I was so much younger, and I remember not really having much of a plan at that point."

I nodded, listening intently as the Prado continued down the dirt road, kicking up a small red dust cloud behind us. "She just needed help… I was in a position to help, even if I was younger than her." Dora listened to the young woman's story and decided that the best course of action would be to bring her home to her mother and get her a bath before finding her a place to stay.

Jumping into action, Dora called her mother to confirm Rose was home. Taking the pregnant woman to her mother's house, Dora introduced the two and quietly asked her mother if she was willing to temporarily house the woman. Despite limited resources, Rose agreed to help that night and work on finding a better solution in the coming days. Prior to going to bed, Dora helped get the young woman cleaned up and settled in for the night. The next day Dora's mother spoke with their pastor to find a permanent solution. They decided she would stay with their family during the day and sleep at the pastor's home. Two weeks later the church community had raised funds to send her home along with money and donated baby clothes.

"I was really glad that what I had done had helped her in a small way," Dora said. "I heard later that she had a healthy baby girl and that her grandmother was able to use the money we raised to start a small business for them." I was beginning to see a pattern in the way Dora connected with people and offered help. Yes, she did downplay her actions, but the most effective thing was her ability to offer small opportunities for people who wanted to help themselves but could not.

The biggest shift in Dora's young adulthood came with her move to Chisamba, a city an hour north of Lusaka. Rose had accepted a job at a Christian mission organization to work at an orphanage. The two moved into a compound occupied by a few missionary families and the children Rose would help care for. Dora was thirteen years old and had just enrolled in a private all-girls boarding school for secondary school. Boarding schools in Zambia are quite common; unlike their European counterparts, they aren't reserved for the extremely affluent. "I loved my school, I felt like I was being challenged more and I was excited to be there," Dora recalled. When speaking with Dora's mother about the type of student Dora was, Rose said, "Dora was intelligent and because of that she could be argumentative… Sometimes people misunderstood her." Whether it was her extensive vocabulary, cumbersome writing, or aspiration to practice law, Dora often felt singled out both in and out of the classroom. The fact that she had such fond memories of her times at school was confusing, another nuance in her personality I was to learn about in greater detail.

When not at school, she returned home to live with her mother in the Christian organization's compound. There, she met the Hamelrycks—an American family with ten children. Dora quickly befriended the entire family. The Hamelrycks came to symbolize not just a family but an entire chapter of

Dora's life. Dora would recount many fond memories of being at their dinner table and on short mission trips together. Over the following years, Dora's relationship with the Hamelrycks deepened as she looked to them for guidance. She spent many days playing with the children and going to church events with the family. Dora referred to the family as her adoptive second family. "They treated me as if I was one of their own daughters. I was at family dinners, and they wanted the best for me too."

Back at high school, Dora enjoyed her classes and had a core group of four friends. But toward the end of her senior year they had a major falling out. She described the culmination of this when three of the friends approached her in the bathroom and began to unload insults over issues in the friend group. "These were my friends. And imagine the hurt. Like I couldn't even defend myself," she said as she recalled them pushing her around and belittling her. After the incident, "my only other friend found me sobbing and crying in the bathroom. And I had been pushed, shoved, and told off and all these things... so yeah... twelfth grade wasn't the best for me. I was losing my... well, I lost my friends."

Although she felt alone in many ways, Dora found purpose through serving others. At the time, she still wanted to pursue a career in law, thinking it would give her the greatest opportunity. Following high school graduation, she spent a year working in Lusaka. She lived in Chisamba and traveled to Lusaka to work at a nonprofit that, through subsidized legal services, helped women escape abusive marriages. Despite the incredible work being done at the organization, Dora realized that law wasn't her path forward. "I wanted to study law, but it would have been Zambian law and I would have had to stay and work here my whole career." Dora aspired to travel and make an impact, but for the time being she was relegated to small-scale projects and organizations she worked at during her free time.

As she contemplated her next step, she took advice from the Hamelyrcks. "They encouraged me to learn a trade such as teaching before trying to be a missionary or starting my own large-scale project." This proved to be extremely practical advice and set Dora down a path that both inspired her and empowered her to begin her journey of impact.

Dora didn't envision her life in this linear path toward her current role. She looked at children like Simon who needed not only a teacher but also an advocate and maternal figure. That person wasn't simply a job that could be summated into an online application or a course offered at a local college. Simon was able to see Dora more clearly than I could. To him, she was truly an individual with skills, abilities, and generosity unlike anyone he had ever encountered. Dora had come into his life for the better. Despite his worsening health, she made every attempt to help him improve. I could only assume he couldn't comprehend why a poor stranger would do that. I also doubt he cared. After all, she never asked for anything in return and continued to help his little body heal. To Simon, Dora was a force for good, something so foreign he probably didn't try to understand it beyond what it was. He likely didn't contemplate the longevity of Dora's funding or the complexity of trying to grow an organization while maintaining current operations. To Simon, Dora served meals starting at 8 a.m. and spent time with him and his classmates every evening before bed. There should be no reason that this ever changed.

For me, it was like trying to solve a puzzle. How did Dora match up to other people I had met and read about? It wasn't that I was trying to fit her into a box; I simply didn't have Simon's childlike capacity to accept her so simply. Dora wasn't a saint. She also wasn't working to benefit herself in any measurable way. Little Simon was a physical reminder that Dora's actions were making a difference. These children wanted to be seen exactly as they were, individuals who wanted to live in a healthier and safer community. The children saw only the positives of the school and how much their lives were improving. Dora, however, needed to balance the fact that the school's future was not guaranteed. The weight of this reality couldn't be seen through her videos, but standing next to her there was no mistaking this truth.

Chapter 4

As Mulilo walked out of the school gates, I felt as though Dora should grab him by the shoulders and shake him back and forth violently. "Do you know what you are giving up? Do you know what opportunity you have in front of you?" Instead, Dora stood by calmly, seemingly unbothered as Mulilo strode out the gate and turned down the road. Every fiber in me wanted to interject, but I also knew there was nothing that could be done. Not only did Dora not have the legal capacity to force Mulilo to stay at the school, but she also knew that wouldn't work in the long run. Mulilo, just ten years old, born to a poor, single mother of four, had decided he no longer wanted an education. His schoolmates had helped him pack up his few belongings, all of which the school had provided, and he was on his way out. Mulilo didn't have any last words for Dora or his classmates. Watching him, I thought he seemed convinced that fending for himself in the village was the best course of action.

"Poverty is a mindset," Dora would often tell me at junctures like this. It was something she is always trying to help others understand. More specifically, me. The idea that someone would reject the tools and opportunities to improve their own lives is difficult for me to comprehend, but it is a phenomenon that Dora deals with every day. She can't help people—even children—who are unwilling or unable to see and accept the value of the support and opportunities she offers. This is a constant point of interest from Dora's online community; her followers ask everything from acceptable questions about economic opportunity all the way to simply blaming Zambians for laziness and ineptitude. Dora herself is often singled out for her role in the situation. At times, she is blamed for her inability to help those who won't accept it, whereas others see her as a savior, doing everything humanly possible to change lives and influence others, perhaps even too much.

Mulilo's home was just a few hundred yards from the school grounds. It was a hot afternoon in late May. I followed Dora as she turned off the main road and down one of the dirt paths toward the village. Two women cooked on a brazier, which is a traditional cooking fire fed by four logs that form a circle and are pushed inward as they burn. The braziers of Kamanda let out a thin trickle of smoke all day and night, never being extinguished. Dora greeted the women cooking as we passed, and they waved in a sympathetic and knowing manner as if they knew where we were heading.

Dora stopped abruptly in front of an open dirt patch where a small cinder block structure was being erected. In the corner of the small plot was a mud hut with a thatched roof. A tattered piece of black plastic had been draped over the apex of the roof. A worn piece of scrap metal served as the front door. Holes had been punched into the metal's right edge and twine tied the "door" to a vertical stick that served as a door frame and hinges. This was Mulilo's home. Stooping to enter, I saw a squalid mattress on the dirt floor. It was pressed up against both walls, taking up more than half the home's single room. Above the bed was a makeshift storage shelf, which housed all the family's possessions. I crouched, making sure not to knock my head against the precarious roof. No one was home.

"How could six people all sleep in here?" I wondered aloud. "The mattress wouldn't even fit me."

Dora responded from the doorway. "Some of them would be on the floor—or maybe outside—while their mother was with a man. But she might also just put up a curtain."

Imagining Mulilo's mother separating the five- by six-foot room with a chitenge cloth to create some perception of privacy before prostituting herself was more than unsettling. Her five children, aged twelve to less than four months old, were no doubt oblivious to the situation in many ways and yet all too aware in others. The claustrophobia-inducing hut was not a place I wanted to stay long. Half a pot of day-old nshima lay in the corner behind the door. It was hard not to wonder how long that food would have to last the mother. Side-stepping around the door, I noticed there was no way to lock it or even keep it permanently shut. I doubted this was a security issue, as even the poorest villagers knew there was nothing of material value to steal.

As we left the hut, Dora began to fill in the details of Mulilo's life. His mother was nearly blind—likely due to cataracts—and could only see shapes and shadows. Before Dora could continue, Vana Mulilo turned the corner. I had never been properly introduced. Dora greeted her before turning to me. I awkwardly bowed and contorted into a curtsy combination. Even after six months in this country, I still was never sure exactly how to greet the village women, as shaking their hands wasn't the norm. I had seen Dora do a similar, albeit more graceful pleasantry, and tried my best to emulate it. Mulilo's youngest brother was slung around his mother's back in a chitenge cloth. Not just in Zambia but across the continent, I had seen these beautifully colorful clothes being used in many ingenious ways. However, seeing a young child nuzzled close to their mother is the most endearing and certainly the cutest. Dora and I were visiting Vana Mulilo because Dora was building her a cinder block house. Vana is a Bemba word meaning mother and is a common way to refer to others through their children's name. Despite building her a house and trying to lift her out of a dire situation, Dora didn't know her real name. It was something that struck me both as very odd but also very indicative of what Dora feels is important. This house would be the first stable home Vana Mulilo would likely ever know.

When explaining her development theory, Dora often cited one of her favorite books on the subject: *When Helping Hurts*.[6] She agreed with the sentiment that development comes with many phases. "There is relief and then there is development. Knowing the difference and when to help is important. Vana Mulilo needs relief first." The book, which Dora read while studying to become a teacher, has strong Christian overtones. Dora warned me of this before I read it but followed up by saying, "The core of what they are getting at is really important and something I think about a lot." I hoped that reading

---

[6] *When Helping Hurts How to Alleviate Poverty without Hurting the Poor...and Yourself* Steve Corbett et al.,| Chicago: Moody Publishers, 2014

the book would help me better understand Dora and why its message resonated so strongly with her. I hoped to unpack the role that religion, specifically Christianity, had played in her past and how it shaped her early worldview. In addition, I was interested in the core topic of the book, which is a highly prescriptive method to alleviate poverty. The author's focus conveyed poverty not only as a material lack of goods, as it is often defined in Western world views, but also as a physiological mindset. Since Dora first read this text, religion's role in her life had diminished greatly. Multiple faiths are practiced and supported at the school, and Dora sees religion as a force in her early life but not a driver of her present or future.

Based on my observations of him at school and among friends, Mulilo seemed to be a quiet and gentle boy. Although I only knew him as a polite and well-mannered child, he had found trouble in his early months at the school. When he first arrived and was welcomed into the boarding house, he found himself in hot water. While unloading groceries for the cafeteria he stole 1000 kwacha (about $50 US) from Dora's purse. Children at the school have no use for money; there is nothing to buy within a forty-five-minute walk in either direction, and even if they could manage to get that far, the only things for sale are vegetables and biscuits. Mulilo was not stealing for himself though; he did it for his mother. Growing up, Mulilo was the man of the house. His mother, unable to do much beyond menial work, sent him out to beg or find work, Dora explained as she inspected Vana Mulilo's new concrete house. Mulilo was the only consistent man in his mother's life and was forced to act well above his age, which undoubtedly took an emotional and psychological toll on him.

"She's how old? I asked, referring to Vana Mulilo.

Dora looked at me. "She's twenty-nine. You can ask Teacher Victor as well."

I would have assumed Vana Mulilo's age to be closing in on forty. Her life was tough, and her body didn't hide that reality. Counting backward, I realized that she was just four years my senior. In many ways, Mulilo grew up with her rather than being raised by her. While pregnant over the last year, Vana Mulilo didn't even have her own pit latrine. The outdoor shower area, which was nothing more than a fenced-in box for privacy, lay derelict in the yard. Meeting Vana Mulilo earlier that week and watching her son from a distance was a reminder of how little I knew about the lives of others. I could see the poverty. It was right in front of me and yet, at the same time, it was a world away.

Mulilo's mother was a prostitute when the opportunity arose, selling herself for food, consumer goods, and paltry amounts. Even upon writing this, it feels somewhat disingenuous, because this seemed as though it was an inconsistent line of work. Around the world, humans exchange sexual favors for drugs, alcohol, food, and myriad other goods. When tied to poverty, which prostitution most often is, the exchange for goods rather than hard currency is a strikingly more desperate act. The result, apart from the physical and emotional toll, were five children. Two young girls and three boys.

While reviewing the hundreds of videos Dora posted since her initial TikTok debut in March 2020, I came across a video of a skinny little boy introducing himself. It was Mulilo, shy and skinnier than the boy I knew. In the video, Dora introduces him and asks him some basic questions. Throughout her social media journey, she has tried to share stories and the impact the school is having. Small, unobtrusive cameos are a way she tries to bring to light the real impact donations have made. Watching this video made two years prior, I could tell that since being at the school, Mulilo's physical health and English had improved dramatically.

The house Dora built was raised with funds from a Go-FundMe. Dora felt compelled to help Vana Mulilo as the mother's options continued to become increasingly limited. When deciding how she would go about helping Vana Mulilo, she spoke to the mother about family planning. Agreeing that bringing another child into the world was not in her or her children's best interest, Vana Mulilo decided to get on long-term contraceptives. This step, Dora felt, was a shift in the right direction. Over the coming weeks, Footprints of Hope had cement bricks shipped in, and a very modest two-bedroom home was erected. Complete with a metal roof, the home was a safe and dry place for the family to reside. Mulilo and the oldest girl, Martha, who was six, would remain in boarding school. "The most shocking part of sharing the home being built were the comments saying how small it was and how there was no bathroom or electricity." It was jarring to hear online commenters share their disappointment in the size or quality of the accommodations. More than anything, it showed their distance from the issue in both understanding and appreciating the natural difficulties of building. Dora's home, indeed the entire school, had no electricity. Running water was a luxury no one had and toilets even more rare. Knowing these truths, the comments still impacted Dora, never ceasing to feel as though they were personal attacks on her efforts.

Later that week as I watched Mulilo leave the school, I stayed silent. I didn't want to disappoint Dora. As hard as I tried, my own upbringing of opportunity and safety prohibited me from accepting Mulilo's rejection of a safe home, warm meals, and a quality education. I sympathized with his predicament but was still angry at his decision to leave. His life up to this point had been filled with pain and challenges, but it had also been extremely free. He was used to making his own decisions and being the proverbial boss. At the school, he suddenly had an enforced bedtime, meals to attend, and classmates who demanded his respect. It wasn't that he resented the school, or the people that loved him—both the teachers and his classmates. It was his inability to cope with structure and discipline that he had never experienced before. For Dora, accepting that not everyone wants help and some people just aren't quite ready to accept help is a key part of creating real change and community impact. In a labored tone of voice, she looked at me and said, "People, even those who development can help the most, are resistant to it because change is cultural."

Despite being frustrated with his shortsightedness, she seemed confident that Mulilo would return. Sitting down that evening, I was no longer angry at the misguided ten-year-old. Mulilo was worthy of everything the school offered him and more. Yet I was frustrated that because of his upbringing, he still made the wrong choice. Like those watching from around the world, I was trying to understand Mulilo's emotions and decisions. I didn't have any knowledge of how they felt. I had no experience with these hardships. I didn't or would never fully be able to understand the effects of poverty as a mindset. Thinking about Mulilo's departure, it was easy to realize the only way to have more empathy was to have more experience.

Dora was working to convert a whole audience that consisted of voyeuristic negative voices and involved onlookers alike. She saw them as equally worthy of gaining an understanding of others from a human point of view. Trying to close the gap between nationalities, income level, and race was a large task. She often fell short. This was to be expected, but her tenacious approach focused on relentless forward movement both in development efforts and in her outreach online. Dora wasn't just concerned with reducing gender violence, forced marriages, water scarcity, poverty alleviation, or access to quality education. Her vision was simpler; transforming the cultural mindset, both the transformation of onlookers via the internet and her physical community of those trapped in the red dust cyclone of poverty in rural Zambia.

Chapter 5

Old friends describe a young woman who made connections with ease, who was headstrong, and who had little time for negativity. Friends described her as someone with "a weakness for sometimes getting too wrapped up in helping others." This was especially true "if you told her she shouldn't or couldn't help."

Experimenting with drugs and alcohol was a waste of time to Dora. Though not against her religion, she really had no interest in that aspect of college life. Dora wanted to spend her time seeking opportunities to engage in community work and interacting with missionaries and teachers. Although she may have differentiated herself socially, she was well accepted and had many friends. Her friend group was diverse, and she made a real effort to fit in at college, which was the first time she had attended a mixed gender school since her primary education.

Education was a natural fit for Dora. She understood the struggle learning posed for many students and the power a quality education could provide. She had dabbled in teaching during her early childhood, sharing her books with others and even starting a nonprofit with three friends to encourage literacy in Lusaka. Although her aspirations to become a lawyer faded, a love for teaching became a more obvious fit for her passion to help others. A three-year teaching college was the next step in her journey.

Back in Mapapa, the Prado struggled to maintain traction on the red sandy soil as I entered a sharp curve. The car then bombed down the center of the road, passing through the vast farmlands. The contrast between the agricultural machinery and small huts never ceased to be a poignant reminder of the economic disparity among those living here. Men and women trudged slowly in the ankle-deep sand to and from work; few owned bicycles, let alone a car or motorcycle. Dora and I were on our way to Mkushi, the nearest city where the school could get resupplied with food and building materials. Dora looked ahead as we talked about her time in college. She was silent for a moment and then asked me if I had dated anyone in college. "Umm yea, I actually dated a woman for a while. She was really nice, but it didn't work out. I was making decisions like a single guy and, well, I guess that caught up to me." We both laughed.

"Constantly moving away isn't the best way to keep someone around, who knew!"

I shrugged as we continued laughing. I returned the question, knowing however that Dora came from a more religious background. I assumed this meant our experiences in the dating world differed greatly.

"I dated a nice German guy a couple years ago, but it didn't work out." She paused and looked out the window and then forward again. "I was raped in college and it's really hard to... well it just... it impacts the way I trust people and date." Dora had been open about her sexual assault in college and worked to help other survivors speak out. To me, however, it was new information.

Unsure of what to say, I spoke honestly. "That's awful... I'm really sorry, Dora. No one should ever go through something like that."

Gracious even in the face of my less than perfect handling of this new information, she began to talk about the impact of her assault. All the while, the car was still slicing through the road onward to Mkushi. She didn't discuss the specifics but talked about her feelings both directly after the assault and now. Somehow, she found ways to be grateful that it wasn't worse. Psychologically, it shifted her life into a before and after. Speaking as though distant from her actual voice, it was clear she had overcome parts of the assault but there were other parts she had not fully healed from. "I used to always be described as bubbly and now even though people see me that way, I'm not sure I actually am."

Fundamentally, her trust in people had been forever altered. Overnight, she had gone from someone filled with a confidence in human beings and the strength of good to a place of doubt. Dora made certain to reiterate that she was the victim. I knew this reiteration was not for me but a reminder to herself. A lesson she was teaching the young girls at the school every day.

The school Dora founded is made up of roughly equal numbers of both genders. The boarding students, however, are overwhelmingly girls. Forced marriage, sexual abuse, and gender-based violence are disproportionally high in rural areas. As such, the girls in the village tend to be at greater risk and therefore a higher percentage of them need housing and protection. The school also has created a grassroots effort within the community to help victims. From an early stage, Dora's vision for her organization was rooted in providing both legal and emotional help to these groups. "Many of these girls only feel safe to speak to someone who has gone through something similar," Dora told me.

Dora was not bold or impassioned when talking about her own story, but it was deeply personal. She treated it in an objective yet emotionally vulnerable manner. When it came to speaking on behalf of the girls and young women she represented, her impassioned voice resonated strongly. As we talked, she slipped into the same natural place I had seen her before. She was in front of a classroom of students. I felt perhaps the same way Mulilo, Nandi, or any of the other 150 students would. I sat in a place of ignorance. Although I had sat in on talks about sexual assault and heard firsthand accounts that resonated strongly, Dora's was different. Our conversation focused not on the incident, but rather its impact.

"I'm not this damaged or a fragile piece of glass, and the look on people's faces when I tell them what happened to me... You can just see how it changes." She retold the way in which others then dismissed her as a sexual being and overlooked her as viable in many ways. As I listened, I noted a hopeful tone in her voice. Despite her experience, she was confident that it would never define her. The clear vision she had for her future and the future of her family was in no way shaped by what had happened to her. Though she knew it was something that altered the way others saw her, she was determined not to let it shape the way her daughters, sons, or future partner would perceive her.

While driving south away from the school after a weeklong visit in August, I brought my blue Toyota Hilux to a shuddering stop when the police flagged me down. Law enforcement checkpoints had become my least favorite thing during these thirteen-hour drives back to my home in Livingstone. Rolling down my window, I could expect one of two things: some brief pleasantries and a wave forward, or a full "inspection," which involved the officer walking around my truck and then reporting that some tiny part of my vehicle was not up to "code." The latter would result in a decision: Do I pay them 100 kwacha on the spot or ask for a receipt, resulting in a legitimate fine being written up with an accompanying 300-kwacha charge? Corruption is a two-way street; it takes good people doing the right thing to combat it as well. This tactic, however, always frustrated me thanks to its enticing nature. Luckily, the officer recognized me from a few days prior. Smiling, he said good afternoon and waved me forward. As I shifted my car into gear, my phone dinged. A voice message had come through. It was a fifteen-minute-long voice message and I knew without even hitting play what it was about.

When Dora and I discussed writing this book, I was hesitant to bring up her sexual assault. Although the topic had been broached in our car ride to Mkushi, the conversation was prior to our decision to write the book. As such, I was asking Dora not to confide in just me, but to also trust me as a writer to handle her story with respect as we shared it with an audience around the world. Nine years before we met, Dora had been assaulted. The lasting emotional and psychological turmoil this did and still does cause her is something no one person could understand. It was something solely she could comprehend.

Rather than waiting until the very end of my research and interview period, I asked Dora at the beginning about including the sexual account. We discussed if this was a portion of her life she felt needed to be shared. She took a short breath inward and said, "Yes, I think if my story can help others, then yes." In this moment of vulnerability, Dora had looked outward to the girls at her school, her daughters, and all the young women watching her online. She is a teacher at heart. Using her own experience, disregarding her own concerns, was the best way for her to teach these students. It just so happened that instead of speaking directly to them she would be sharing this story and teaching with me.

I pulled my car to the side of the highway, a two-lane road riddled with potholes. Large semi-trucks seemed to shake the earth as they careened past at speeds that seemed uncontrollable on these poor roads. Before I hit play, I braced myself.

Whatever I heard on this recording I was going to have to write about. Dora had entrusted me with an enormous responsibility to share her story. The way in which I handled it was critical to someone I admired and wanted to treat with the utmost respect.

Dora had recorded it late at night, her daughters, all five of them, fast asleep just down the hall. The voice that spoke out was soft, almost a whisper. She began.

"I was in college... I was still a virgin."

Pausing, she continued slowly. *"When I went to college, everybody had boyfriends. It was like a switch was flipped and overnight everyone was seeing someone."* Dora's observation came across as just that; her tone lacked any judgment. *"One evening, while walking home after studying with a housemate of mine, we ran into a group of young men. They were gathered by our house trying to fix the pool. As we passed, they started catcalling us and trying to get our attention."* She broke from the narrative tone. *"I hate when that happens. Like I really hate it."* Transitioning back to her story, Dora said, *"The friend I was with was sort of basking in these 'compliments.' I was just like, 'Come on, let's just go.'"*

One of the young men approached the two girls. He was young and good looking, in part to many because he was biracial. Colorism was something Dora often pointed out and addressed at the school and in her own life. When reflecting on the young man, she was aware of his relative position in the social hierarchy thanks to his lighter skin tone. *"As this young biracial man approached us he spoke up and said, 'Hey, ladies, how are you?'"* Dora told her friend that she was tired and was going to bed. It was a polite excuse to remove herself from an uncomfortable situation. Her friend remained with the boys and continued chatting. Prior to his leaving, the young biracial man asked her friend for Dora's number. Her friend gave it to him, unbeknownst to Dora. *"Just as I was getting into the apartment, my friend caught up to me. She explained that the guys seemed harmless and told me that she had given my number to the biracial boy."* Dora was naturally upset at this breach of privacy and shared her displeasure with her friend. *"Really? You shouldn't have done that. You didn't ask me. I left that conversation for a reason."* Over the following week, the young man began to text and call Dora. *"He began texting and calling me daily. He didn't exactly say much, he would just ask 'hey what's up?' and 'Can I come and visit?'"* Over the course of the week he continued to visit the boarding house and eventually asked Dora on a date. *"When he asked me on a date I accepted. I didn't see what I had to lose. It was just a date, right?"*

Over the course of the following weeks the two began to get to know one another. *"We went out on a date. It was alright, nothing really special or memorable. He asked me out again and again. Our second date was okay. We continued to go out, three, four, five dates and we still didn't get physical. He didn't have the characteristics that I knew I wanted in a boyfriend. But there was a lot of pressure from my housemates and my friends. They were always commenting on how handsome he was or that he was biracial and how special that was. One day he asked me to go out at night to a club with him. I was very hesitant, because that wasn't a place I went or was comfortable going necessarily. By then, however, he had come over to the boarding house with his friends as well as different girls. It seemed like there was a greater group; it wouldn't just be the two of us."* Collective pressure to fit in and a desire to get away from her studies combined and Dora decided to join them. *"He reassured me before going by saying, 'Don't worry, your friends are also coming. You can come and still be Dora.' I agreed, thinking I would be safe as long as my friends were around."*

Dora wasn't a drinker and her friends knew this. In the club that night she didn't face any pressure to consume alcohol. *"At the time I was strict about not drinking, which also meant I didn't have any understanding of drinking safety. I ordered a Fruittree juice... I had no idea that regardless of there being alcohol you should be careful and watch your drink."* Unaware that someone could potentially drug her drink, Dora began dancing. *"I was enjoying the music, I was dancing with friends and then stepped away to use the bathroom. When I came back, I took the same juice not even thinking someone could have drugged me."* Just a few minutes later, Dora began to feel sick and realized things were not right with her body. *"At first I just thought I was sick, but it was more than that. I needed to go home really badly. I had no idea what was going on."* Dora's date and his friends took it upon themselves to escort the girls home. *"At this point the girls were all quite badly drunk. Many of the girls had been sleeping with their boyfriends, so it wasn't odd for us to separate quickly."*

At this point her voice changed. She sounded more distant, as if she had forgotten that the recording was still on. *"I was brought into my room and I tried to say goodbye... I don't remember it very well..."* She trailed off. *"Instead of leaving he closed the door and basically said, 'I'm not going. Every time we go out, we do nothing. Nothing happens. It's my day to do something.'"* Recalling the assault, it's clear to Dora that she was drugged that night. At the time she was unaware that this danger existed, regardless of whether she had consumed alcohol. She thought she had been extremely cautious at the club, but she now found herself in a dire situation. *"I was feeling extremely dizzy and was still trying to push him away and fight him off. He wouldn't budge. He pushed me hard and I fell back, hitting my head. The back of my head began to bleed and that's the last thing I remember."*

Concerned about Dora's well-being, a friend came to Dora's house after not receiving word from her over text. *"I was bloody... My head felt like it was going to blow up. And then when I told her what I remembered, I began to realize exactly what had happened. I was in shock."* Unsure of what action to take, the friend advised Dora to bathe before going to the police station. *"My friend told me that we needed to see the police but that I couldn't walk around in my bloody state. She advised me to take a bath and clean up before we went to get help."* Dora, unaware that bathing after an assault would reduce the likelihood of police finding DNA, agreed that bathing was the right thing to do. The two then went to the police station, both very emotionally unnerved and unsure about the reception they would receive from law enforcement. *"The police were pretty calm. They listened to us, but didn't believe our story. The police simply didn't believe this happened to me. After that my friend and I went to the clinic hoping to get help there. The people at the clinic also didn't believe me. I was told that if this had really happened the only thing I could do was to sue the party responsible."*

Dora then made the most difficult decision; she chose to go in front of a judge and relive that night. *"I decided to go to court and try to get justice for myself. Unfortunately, because I bathed the morning after the assault, the clinic wasn't able to find any residual blood or DNA. This was a big reason I lost the case... I lost the case and he won."* I could hear the deadness in her voice, totally removed from the moment she was currently living.

She was back in the courtroom hearing that even the justice system of Zambia didn't believe her. *"The judge ruled in favor of the defendant. I was told that it was clear we were dating and it was as if we just had sex. Those that were a part of the court proceedings kept saying I can't go after him for having sex with me. They just saw him as my boyfriend. 'Stuff like this happens' was something I heard a lot. I was extremely emotional, because these people didn't understand. This happened to me. I didn't have any power or part in the decision."*

Dora's story is one of thousands that pass through the Zambian court system every year. Even more go unreported. It's a part of her life that shaped her empathy for young girls, who, like her, had no advocate. *"That's my story, I lost. He walked and I was... I was left to pick up the pieces. It's a part of my life but it doesn't define me."* Observing Dora, it's impossible to comprehend the exact ways in which her assault impacts her. I, like all her students, only see the woman standing in front of the room. Teacher Dora, the young black Zambian woman, using her experiences to educate and inspire others.

Chapter 6

Teacher Victor signaled me to continue backing up my pickup truck. I had parked in front of the school's silver passenger van and we needed both vehicles that morning. The van, which had been donated anonymously, enabled the school to expand their reach and help educate students who lived deeper into the bush. Victor climbed into the van and pulled ahead of me. We both drove up to the main classroom block and parked momentarily. Children began to climb into both the van and my truck. Two minutes later there were ten people in my two-door truck that had seatbelts for four. It reminded me of one of Dora's favorite jokes. "How many people fit in an African taxi? One more!" It was this mentality of "one more" that she also seemed to bring to the school. How many kids can we feed, clothe, and educate? One more.

A long day of work awaited us. In the months leading up the rainy season, the teachers and staff had planted soybeans in a few open fields. It was now time to harvest the beans and, like all the villagers, we had no machinery. Victor and I ferried students to the fields where teachers awaited them. Once there, everyone pitched in and began to pick the beans and pile them into enormous heaps. Victor and I then used my truck and the van to shuttle the harvest back to the school. Always thinking ahead, Dora was concerned about the money needed to run the school, and this was a way to become more sustainable. If the price of soybeans was high the school would sell them; if it was low, they would process the beans themselves for their own consumption.

The students were happy to be outside for the day enjoying the cool breeze and joking around with one another. As the afternoon came to a close Dora and I began talking about her post-college years. She looked back on those years fondly as they had been spent with people she felt understood her. Given her mother's South African roots, Dora often spoke about identifying as a "third culture kid," someone who was never quite at home in her mother country but also lacked the identity of another nation. During her post-college years she spent an increasing amount of time with people who knew those feelings intimately: foreign missionaries.

After getting her diploma from teaching college it was time for Dora to set about finding a job. Passionate about helping others, she began to speak openly about her vision of someday opening her own school. Without professional experience and in need of work, she spoke to the Hamelrycks about becoming a missionary. "From very early on in my life I felt this need. I wanted to help others and make that my life's work. Going to teaching college and then becoming a missionary were steps on that journey." Seeing in her a passion to help others and spread Christianity, the Hamelrycks supported Dora's ambition. During the following year she took classes and learned about the various components in becoming a foreign missionary. Over the course of that year Dora took on her most ambitious project: starting a small school for the children of deaf parents who attended her church. Many of the children did not have impaired hearing; however, their education had suffered due to the lack of verbal communication at home. Dora made many of her first breakthroughs as a teacher during this period.

Socially, Dora had many friends both in and outside of work. One person in particular, Ashley Keller, stood out and became a mentor and longtime friend. The two met through the Hamelrycks.

"Age wise I fell between the mom and the kids," Ashley recalled, "so sometimes I would be with the older {Hamelryck children} whom Dora was also friends with or spending time with the mom." Through this mutual connection the two became fast friends. Ashley, an American, had met her husband, also an American, while on a gap year in Zambia. She decided to stay in Zambia and join her husband who was doing humanitarian work. Between the responsibilities of raising children and the gatekeeping of others, Ashley's personal projects had become stalled. "Dora, from the start, was just like we can do this!" and a natural partnership was born. Dora, who loved interacting with children, soon became part of the Keller family. Speaking with Ashley about this time, the love that Dora felt for her children and the Keller family was evident. In conversation Dora was clear about Ashley's influence as a mentor and friend.

The laptop's dim glow lit up my face that evening as I hunched over my keypad. Zambia, despite what many people think, gets quite cold during the winter. High thirties and low forties are common at night and feel even more wicked when your blood is used to the hot African sun. I was on a short sectional couch in the front room of the cinder block guest home, tucked away in a section of trees near the back end of the school, just opposite Teacher Dora's house. The structure was not yet complete and as such rats had invaded the apex of the metal roof and could be heard scurrying above my bed during the night. This evening, however, I was more preoccupied with trying to place my Wi-Fi receiver in the precise spot to get just barely enough network to Skype call Ashley Keller. The meeting began to dial and Ashley appeared on screen. She was at a swim meet and had stepped out into the parking lot.

Researching Dora's life was challenging. Many people in mission work, unsure of my motives, were hesitant to speak to me as an outsider. Others, though happy to speak to me, perhaps only shared the positive aspects of Dora and her accomplishments. Getting beyond the surface of Dora was tricky. "Yea, Dora had a lot of negative voices in her life at the time, people saying she was above mission and why would you help these people? Or what makes you think you should travel the world?" This was the first time I had heard someone directly addressing the doubters and emotional scars evident in Dora's self-confidence.

After finishing her mission training and final project, Dora was unsure what was next. For a time she was adrift, working odd jobs to bring in enough money while doing mission work. "Dora was never above a job no matter how menial it was. She would just step in and start," Ashely recalled. I remembered that

Dora had once told me that she viewed "money as just money. It doesn't matter what job I worked to get it, as long as it kept me headed in the direction of my goals." It was this inch-by-inch mentality she used as self-preservation during some of the slow periods of tangible growth during those early years.

In speaking with others about Dora's early years in mission work, it was clear to me that she faced many challenges. Dora was a black Zambian woman in a world dominated by well-educated foreigners. Many if not all missionaries and NGO employees were highly educated white people with years of experience abroad. Dora, with her Zambian teaching certificate and social status, was knocking at a cinder block wall without a door. Some of these challenges were perceived as social constructs whereas others were legitimate reasons as to why she was not being chosen for greater tasks. "When I met Dora she had atrocious grammar and spelling. She would write and I would just be like, I can't help you publish this," Ashley recalled. For me as a foreigner, the extent to which education differs around the world is hard to decipher. I often wanted to ignore signs contrary to the rosy depiction of higher education in Zambia, but I knew that wasn't being honest. This was difficult because over the year, I had come to have a deep respect and admiration for the Zambian people.

Ignoring the educational gap, however, would be a disservice to Dora's accomplishments and her many Zambian contemporaries. Zambian education varies greatly by region. National statistics report that 91 percent of children graduate grade 7. However, the level of English language competence, the language in which all classes are taught, is highly debatable. Daily, I struggled with self-proclaimed "English speakers" who had received their higher education in Zambia. Many of them had difficulty getting past basic conversation. This is a country that had 109 college graduates upon getting their independence in 1964. Colonialism's hangover in Zambia is the main reason why foreigners play a large role in the major industries throughout the nation. There remains a wide educational and subsequent knowledge gap between foreigners and native Zambians. Subject to 'brain drain' many of Zambia's best and brightest leave the country for greener pastures when given the opportunity.

When I addressed this directly with Dora, she was rightly insecure about this part of her journey. She had achieved so much, only to be brought back to some of the toughest challenges she faced. "I was always a very strong reader," she said, looking ahead, clearly frustrated by my prying. I immediately regretted trying to distinguish educational standards. It was no doubt something she had dealt with others doing her whole life. My goal was to highlight her strength in overcoming these challenges, but it was obvious that Dora felt I had no understanding of the educational differences. Ashley recalled the initial strength it took Dora to come to the realization that a foreigner without a college degree had come to her and said, "Your writing isn't good enough." Dora was younger than the people around her and felt the pressure at every turn. But instead of folding she decided to tackle this deficiency.

As I sat in the cold cinder block room on my video call with Ashley, I heard the first retelling of Dora's additional education. The two sat huddled over homeschooling books in the Keller's kitchen, slowly building Dora's skills and confidence. Often, when hearing about Dora's insecurities and how others had injured her, I realized the extent to which Dora still guarded herself from others. We had spent many hours together at this point, but despite our relative closeness she was still self-protective. This, and subsequent conversations with others, only deepened my respect for a woman whom I already knew faced enormous challenges.

"Dora was coming to the realization that she deserved a place at the table," Ashley concluded, as we were talking about this chapter of Dora's journey. I wondered if Dora truly internalized that feeling. To me, she was still chronically humble and doubtful of the power she possessed. While writing this book, I got a text message from her about a question I sent and she said, "Are you sure you want to write this book about me? Like is there even enough?" Having already written half the book and spent months on the project, her questions were a bit jarring. It was also a perfect indicator of her distinct belief she was not worthy. Dora had at the age of twenty-two learned how to write in a professional manner. It took a great deal of humility to relearn and accept that her own weaknesses potentially held her back.

During the end of this period Dora saw a Facebook post that would dramatically alter her course. Two missionaries were rescuing young Dalit women on the outskirts of Chennai, a major city in India. Once referred to as the untouchables, the Dalit are found at the bottom of the ethnographic caste system of India. "The Dalit female belongs to the most oppressed group in the world," says Dr Suraj Yengde, author of *Caste Matters*.[7] For the first time in her life Dora was now reading about a group of women on another continent up against an enormous social system similar but incomparable to the one she battled in Zambia. "I had empathy when I learned about these women because I was always the darker one," Dora recalled, referring to her own challenges of colorism among Zambians and racism in the broader spectrum. "I felt a burden in my heart learning about their struggles and felt that I was called to make this my

[7] *Caste Matters,* Suraj Yengde and Cornel West (Gurgaon, India: Penguin Viking, 2019)

life. I knew I had to move to India." Dora was compelled to find a way to be a part of what she described as her "calling."

Mutual friends of the Kellers spoke with Dora. From the beginning, Dora knew that she would have to raise funds to realize her goal of moving to India. Impassioned by the idea of helping a group of young women, Dora set to work. She spoke to others about her goal and began raising funds. Nearing the deadline of the opportunity to join the team working in India, word came through of an anonymous donation. "I was overwhelmed when I found out," she recalled, saying that it was the realization of everything she had been working toward.

Landing in India, the heat first hit Dora, then the smells and sights of a place so culturally foreign from her own. Over the course of the following months Dora would become integrated into the ongoing mission and humanitarian work with the young Dalit women. Outside Chennai, a city of five million, Dora was finding her footing around her changing worldview. The leaders of the organization were a young couple. Dora admired them for their tenacity at tackling some of the most difficult issues facing India's most vulnerable people. Paul, the husband, was Indian by birth and Molly, his wife, had been raised in America. The two helped shape Dora's vision of what could be accomplished in a short period of time when applying yourself to a mission with a deep personal meaning.

As she spent the following year and a half in and out of India, Dora's dream of starting her own school only grew.

Mentoring and caring for the young Dalit women, Dora forged deep relationships and her perspective began to shift. Although her initial plan when coming to India was to stay long term, after just a year she began to think about her home country. Zambia was a young nation facing many problems, many of which Dora felt personally compelled to help solve. "I came to realize that Zambia had an enormous need and that's why I wanted to return." Need was something Dora often spoke about in regard to how she perceived what she would work on the rest of her life. "In Zambia I knew that I would be more effective, and the need was so great that I felt it was time to return to start on a new journey." After over a year and a half spent in India with some of the world's most vulnerable women, Dora moved back home to Zambia. The decision cemented her commitment to the nation and its future.

Need seems very simple to understand in Zambia and in many other parts of Africa. Aid would also seem to be very simple; however, the concept of aid has proven complex. African aid is certainly not new, dating back as far as 1896 and becoming even clearer post–World War II and specifically involving the Marshall Plan in the 1950s.[8] At the turn of the

---

[8] Britannica, The Editors of Encyclopaedia. "Marshall Plan". *Encyclopedia Britannica*, 24 Nov. 2022

century, the notion that foreign aid was the only solution to the multiple problems facing the poorest countries of Africa took root. From 1950–2000 over two trillion dollars was transferred from rich countries to poor, with Africa receiving the bulk of that money.[9] Many have argued it simply has not worked. Leaders of many countries have lost or stayed in power depending on how they managed aid and how they aligned themselves with those who distributed the aid. How best to use foreign money or if foreign money is part of the solution remains debatable among those who best understand the economics of the poorest of the African countries. Although aid remains complex and without a clear path, need remains unquestioned.

Returning home from India, Dora slotted back into her old life. She was busy spending time with the Kellers, starting work at a mission organization, and taking steps toward her dream of starting a school. Professionally, her time in India as a foreign missionary opened doors. Landing a job as the personal assistant to the director of a mission organization, Dora gained a front row seat to understanding how a large NGO was run. She would eventually use this education to run her own organization. "In many ways I am really grateful for all I learned from my missionary work despite eventually

---

[9] World Bank, Net official development assistance and official aid received, Dec. 2020

going in a different direction." During years of working with a highly funded organization, Dora was able to cut her teeth as an aspiring leader. While making strides within the organization she was presented with an opportunity to further her education. Though a licensed teacher in Zambia, she lacked international certification. The missionary organization offered to loan her school funds if she was accepted into a program that specialized in teaching English as a foreign language.

CELTA and DELTA would be Dora's goals for the next year as she looked at achieving her highest level of formal education. CELTA is a specific brand certificate in English Language Teaching awarded by the University of Cambridge's nonprofit assessment organization, the Cambridge English Assessment. The course is offered by a variety of schools and educational institutions. It is the equivalent of an intensive 120-hour TEFL certification and trains you to teach English to adults only.[10] DELTA stands for Diploma in English Language Teaching to Adults. Like CELTA, DELTA is another certification brand awarded by Cambridge English Assessment but is more restrictive in that it is only offered to qualified teachers. Combined, it commonly takes students six months to a year to complete the course in a distanced learning or part-time capacity.

"Hell on earth," Thandiwe blurted out when I asked Dora

---

[10] English Language Assessment, Cambridge University Press 2022

to describe her experience during the Cambridge course. The three of us, driving back to the school after a two-hour supply run to Kapiri, all began to laugh. It was true that Dora struggled significantly during the course. Dora's friend Ashley reminded me that Dora had never completed a rigorous Western-style course before and quickly found it was intense and consumed all her energy. While taking the course, Dora was still working full time at the mission organization and taking on mounting responsibilities. When she finally arrived at the in-person sessions she felt as though she had been thrown in the deep end. "I felt singled out from the beginning. I was the youngest by a lot in our class and the only black person... Preference was definitely given to other students who had better relationships with the professors." Dora found it hard to maintain a cheery attitude and to win over professors she felt wanted to see her fail. "It was really difficult, and I just felt like at every turn I wasn't good enough." During the final weeks of the session the teachers met in South Africa to do in-person teaching assessments. "I failed a section and I knew that meant I was likely going to fail the whole course. I went to the bathroom and just broke down... I had an adult panic attack. I called Ashley but she was driving and didn't answer." Finally, Dora got through to Ashley's husband, Tim. He helped calm Dora down and got Ashley on a conference call. "They told me that they would fly me home that night and we could just figure out a way for me to retake the course. That it was okay. I hadn't failed, it just wasn't going to happen this time." At this point others in the class had realized what was happening. Some students had dropped out earlier, but a core group had remained and become close. While encouraging words were spoken to her through a bathroom stall door, Dora reassessed. "I told the Kellers I was going to keep going and I would rather fail than stop trying." Dora was given another chance at a critical stage by professors she felt "had realized how tough they were being on me" and passed the course. Upon completion, she was not overly excited or proud, but exhausted. Emotionally drained from the previous weeks, Dora was relieved to have this major hurdle behind her.

"Mwashibukeni!" I called out as I walked across the sand yard separating the guest house from Dora's cinder block home. It was a cool morning; dew covered the crooked front window. From inside the kitchen a roar of giggles erupted. Six of Dora's children sat in the kitchen waiting for their breakfast. While at the school I made a point to only use the two or three Bemba phrases with people whom I knew spoke English. As mentioned earlier, the school had a strict No Bemba rule to immerse the children in an English learning environment. Dora's daughters, however, thought my accent and mispronunciation of the words was a riot. Filing out of the kitchen from shortest to tallest, they trotted to the wooden picnic table. A metal roof protruded out of the green painted home and a polished and slippery concrete floor was underfoot. The family's two dogs jumped excitedly at me as I joined the girls at the table.

With only a primary school currently built at Footprints of Hope, it was not yet possible to educate all her children close to home, which was why three of Dora's other children were attending boarding school. It was common in the evening to hear the girls speaking with their siblings loudly over speakerphone. Exclamations at the youngest girl's improving English vocabulary were always followed by proud smiles. The Nyambe clan is a mismatched group of ages, personalities, and skin tones. Despite their differences, the girls are particularly close. Dora, like all parents, has many concerns about their future. Cultural beauty standards in Zambia and the impact on her daughters and girls at the school give her anxiety.

At a young age Dora was distinctly aware of her dark skin. Zambia's population is overwhelmingly black. Of the eighteen million citizens, it's estimated around forty thousand are white, eighty thousand Chinese, and fifteen thousand of Indian descent. Colorism, or preferential treatment based on skin tones, remains an issue. Differing from racism, colorism is propagated by the black majority rather than a foreign race. Likely a cultural legacy of colonialism and the perceived international beauty standard, colorism is a detriment to equal treatment among peoples and specifically among women. "Light skin in Zambia is just seen as way more desirable. A lot of young girls use bleaching and whitening creams," Dora relayed to me.

Dora, seemingly always on the move, needed to drive south three hours to Kabwe. A slow trickle of donation packages arrives from around the world monthly. Each donation is precious, often packed with supplies the school either can't access locally or simply can't afford. Containing items such as educational posters, colored pencils, and multiple copies of the same book for teaching purposes, the packages are eagerly anticipated by everyone. Dora stepped out of the house and as standard procedure was showered with compliments from her daughters. She aptly returned them, a round of daily affirmation that everyone in the school participates in throughout the day. Oftentimes, at my most sleep-deprived and scruffy moments, the students somehow snuck in a compliment. It was an endearing and practical use of their growing English skills.

The girls all waved goodbye as I pulled the Prado out of

the sand and onto the gravel road running through the school grounds. The first hour of our drive to Kabwe was the most difficult. As we bobbed up and down it felt as though we were riding over downed trees rather than compressed dirt. The car labored forward, and Dora began to reflect on Kabwe, a city where she spent much of her adult life. After college she worked there as a missionary and developed friendships with many locals. More importantly, Kabwe was where she met Veronica, her first adopted daughter.

In 2016, Dora was a twenty-four-year-old working and living in a mid-size Zambian city. She had a small but comfortable apartment. Missionary work did not pay a normal salary, so Dora worked and raised funds to support herself. Although she was far from financially secure, she had enough funds to support herself. On a cloudy Tuesday morning, Dora was getting ready for work when she heard a knock on the door. A teenage girl stood at the door and asked Dora if she had any laundry or work that she could do. Dora, confused as to why the girl was working and not in school, began to question her. During this initial conversation, it was clear to Dora that Veronica had a disability, likely mild autism. Veronica explained her home situation; at the time, she was living with an aunt who forced her each day to look for work. Unnerved, Dora stepped out of the house and asked Veronica if she would like to attend school. Veronica, looking at the ground, responded softly that she was unable to afford school fees. Dora told her to return that evening with her aunt and they would have a discussion.

The decision to adopt Veronica was based on the girl's need for a safe home. Dora did little to assess how this decision would impact her own life. "There was this girl standing in front of me who needed help and I had the capacity to help. It didn't seem like there was any other decision to make." She said this to me as if it was as rational as the need to fill the Prado with gas rather than diesel.

"Dora didn't stop to think, Is adopting a teenager with a traumatic past the simplest way to ease myself into fostering and adopting?" Ashley recalled when we spoke about her impression of Dora's decision. "Capacity to help" remains a relative concept to Dora. At the time, her own future was very uncertain. Those around her felt she was perhaps being compulsive. She was. Dora is compelled to help, not to watch or comment. She jumps at every chance to meaningfully act when she can leverage her own abilities and gifts.

Raising Veronica would prove to be a challenge. Dora often had difficulty setting boundaries with her, and at times she would run back to her relatives. Like many of the children now at Footprints of Hope, stability was foreign and constrictive. As the challenges continued, Dora poured herself into the role of mother. I couldn't help but think about how close in age Dora is to Veronica. Separated by only a decade, Dora was forced to mature even more quickly than most young mothers. It is one thing to parent a helpless baby or a toddler who hasn't quite discovered the concept of autonomy, but quite another to raise a strong-willed teenager who had never experienced supportive structure and discipline.

After almost a year of caring for Veronica, Dora adopted again. This time it was a relative of Veronica's, another girl in need of a safe place to live. Focusing on their education, Dora worked to get the girls enrolled in private school and help them recoup the years lost while they were neglected.

Adoption, like many institutions in Zambia, is a government construct of sorts. The common Western view of adoption in which an individual is granted full and permanent parental rights and legal guardianship does exist in Zambia, but it has a cost and litany of legal requirements. Dora, with her meager financial means, had little opportunity to secure the full legal rights that a traditional adoptive parent would have. As such, she worked within the Zambian legal framework to gain guardianship. This guardianship enabled Dora to legally raise the girls away from their relatives. It was clear throughout her explanation of the maze of legal hoops she was continually forced to jump through, that it had caused her some mental distress. Eventually, however, Dora became the mother of twelve children.

While I continued driving, Dora began to unload the pressures of this tenuous legal status. It was clear that in the eyes of the Zambian government she was doing the right thing, caring for and loving twelve children. Unfortunately, the social worker's opinions would have little weight if any of the extended family members of Dora's children came forward to demand greater legal rights. This is a fear Dora lives with constantly. Her youngest, Sylvia, a shy toddler full of coy smiles and waves, has never known another mother. Dora couldn't bear the thought of being separated from her. To her, and the children, they are a family. The girls have even gone so far as to ask their mother to change their last name to share hers. Dora and her daughters truly are the Nyambe family.

Our discussion of Dora's adoptive children was a topic she was nervous to speak about openly. To the world she was a mother, NGO director, and compassionate humanitarian. She proudly shared with her online audience the fact that she has adopted twelve children. Privately though, she confided her concern that others would see her legal status and assume she was less of a mother. This concern and her limited legal rights highlighted her commitment to the Nyambe family even more poignantly. Dora cared little that she might never have the full legal right of refusal if extended family members wanted visitation rights. She was her children's mother, the matriarch of the family.

Mercifully, the dirt road ended and I pulled onto the two-lane highway stretching south. On the tarmac the rattling noise of the car quieted, as did our conversation. "Is cultural change tied to the development of Mapapa?" I asked.

Dora paused before answering. "Along with development in Mapapa the culture also needs to change. So both, they happen together."

It was a topic I thought about often, how Dora's impact on the youth of Mapapa would change the landscape of their village. Across the nation as young people became more educated, they flooded the cities and left traditional livelihoods and customs behind. Brain drain, as it is often referred to, was leaving many rural areas bereft of educated leaders.

"Do you know what pulling is?" Dora asked somewhat coyly. She explained it is a cultural practice among women. Discussed behind closed doors, it is the act of stretching a woman's labia minora. "Pulling" is often promulgated by matriarchs of the family, the practice typically beginning at the age of ten. "My mother is South African so it wasn't something we ever talked about. But I knew my friends were doing it and others were being pressured to." Excruciatingly painful, this form of genital mutilation is seen to serve multiple purposes. Increasing male sexual pleasure, easing the pain of childbirth, and cultural homogeneity are excuses given to the widespread but rarely discussed practice.[11] Whether she fully conceptualized it, Dora was working to create a Zambia that she herself would have been safer and more prosperous in. Every girl she taught at school and each daughter she raised would add to this cultural shift. This shift was not away from a traditional Zambian identity, but rather one that embraced all Zambians, specifically the gender that had been left behind.

Arriving in Kabwe, we stopped at the post office and picked up the packages. There were six in total. Dora was beaming as we carried them to the car. Seeing her navigate the streets of Kabwe, ducking into stalls and conversing with women at the market, it was clear this was home. Not necessarily Kabwe itself, but here among other Zambians. Collectively they were part of a whole, working with one another on a busy afternoon. I felt these people knew how special she was. Dora is Zambian in the same way the Zambezi River, which flows down the country's western border is "Zambian." Like Dora, the river crosses into different nations, influenced by many nationalities, but has over time become a Zambian entity. Dora represents

---

[11] Zambian Girls Stretch Labia to Avoid Infidelity, Global Press Journal, Chanda Katongo July 30, 2013

the best of what a Zambian woman could be. Watching the kinship among her and the Zambians was like the relationship of the river with those living on its banks. Everyday citizens, even those unaware of the international fame or power of Dora or the river, had natural respect for both.

Chapter 7

"Village Duck!" Dora exclaimed, turning to me with raised eyebrows and a wide smile. Despite the phone pressed to her ear, I could still make out a faint voice on the other line. William Mushanga spoke slowly, telling Dora he looked forward to seeing her and me this evening. Mushanga was Dora's "village father" of sorts. In early 2019, Alina, a friend of Dora's, brought her to Mapapa to visit her family. This unassuming trip to see a friend's family and learn more about traditional village life would become a catalyst of Dora's long-term development goals. Curious to speak with the family that had first shown Dora around her future home, I asked Dora to arrange a meeting. Hours later it was settled; we would be sharing a meal with the Mushanga family that evening.

Mapapa is an easy place to miss. A collection of five cinder block shops face the road. Painted white but stained beige from the relentless dust, the shops do little to differentiate Mapapa from the other twenty villages within an hour's drive. An abandoned building that has begun to crumble has "Mapapa Police" written on its side. It is the only indication that Mapapa exists beyond word of mouth.

As the Prado turned down the road, which was designed for pedestrians and not the wide 4x4 body of the Toyota, children stared and pointed at me. Dora rolled down her window and motioned for me to stop. A man approached the car, greeting Dora, then Thandiwe, and finally me. Smiling as he spoke in Bemba, it was clear he was sharing his appreciation for them. Others came closer to exchange words of thanks with the two women. Children who saw my companions felt emboldened to wave and call out in English, giggling as they did so. It was a pleasant winter evening. The setting sun struck the straw roofs at an angle, making them golden brown. Dora absent-mindedly gave directions, forgetting that I had little idea of where I was. Shortly she realized I had made a wrong turn. With only two paths for options, it was a comical error. Unable to turn around due to the width of the road, we reversed a few hundred feet and resumed.

The Mushangas' home stood out prominently with its metal

roof. Construction materials were a practical indicator of a family's financial means. In Mapapa there are three dominant styles of buildings: mud, burnt bricks, and cinder blocks. Mud homes are the least expensive to make, though this doesn't make them simple to build or maintain. The most prevalent style of construction in this part of Zambia is burnt bricks. These are rectangles molded out of mud, dried, and then fired in a clay oven. The result is a homemade brick, sturdy and easy to build with. Although a cost-effective method, they have a reputation for eroding quickly and thus can be hazardous as buildings give way. Cinder blocks are the preferred option but also the most cost restrictive—in many small villages, only businesses, schools, and churches can afford them. The day we drove through Mapapa, I didn't see a single house built with cinder blocks.

Roofs play a similar role in providing a rough benchmark of the developmental stage of an area. Again, three main categories create distinctions between villagers. There are thatched roofs, exposed tin roofs, and insulated tin roofs. The thatched roofs were created with tightly bundling up material found naturally around the village prior to laying it atop the hut. This is done similar to how a shingle or tin roof would be laid. Creating a thatched roof is truly a craft of its own. While driving in the rural areas, often I would see beautiful patterns of tightly woven thatched roofs. These roofs, however, have many downsides, the greatest being flammability. Bush fires are common during the dry season. I heard many stories of villagers who died, unable to escape their home quickly enough when the roof caught fire. Other issues included leaks, maintenance, and pests entering through gaps in the roof. Tin roofs solve many of these problems but for most are far too expensive. The greatest luxury among these tin roof options are insulated roofs. This is accomplished by hiding the rafters that hold up the roof with another sheet of metal or wood and inserting insulation. Throughout my time in Zambia I never saw an insulated roof in a village.

Stepping out of the car, I surveyed the yard as villagers watched the three of us approach the house. William Mushanga greeted us at the doorway, shaking my hand before leading me inside. Upon entering the home I saw a small square room that connected the three rooms, each doorway covered with a sheet. Pushing the curtain aside, I entered the living room. Light flooded in from a single glass window, about shoulder height. The tall ceilings made the home feel open, despite being no more than fifteen by eight feet. Mushanga sat down on an orange plastic chair opposite the window. The floor was compacted earth, visible through gaps in the patchwork of vinyl plastic mats lining the floor. Electrical wires trailed vertically down from the roof and connected to a small in-verter. Although it looked old and perhaps broken, a green light still flickered. Clasping his hands, Mushanga once again welcomed us to his home.

In early 2019 Dora had never heard of Mapapa; in fact, she no longer planned to live in Zambia. After finishing CELTA and DELTA she continued to make strides as an educator. Her consistent effort to improve her English writing and teaching skills were beginning to pay off. Offers from private schools and foreign teaching jobs were now real opportunities Dora could take advantage of. From a financial standpoint, these were lucrative jobs compared to the work she was currently doing. Because she had little in the way of savings, many people were surprised that she didn't jump at the first opportunity that came along. But at the time, regardless of money, Dora felt her work in rural undeveloped areas was simply more important.

During this time, another two girls came into her life, growing her family from three to five. Contemplating her next steps, a chance to teach in China became a reality. "I justified it by telling myself that the money would allow me to support the girls and potentially other adoptions or even pay someone to set up a small school." The desire to run her own school was a dream she felt was quickly passing her by. "In a lot of ways, I think Dora thought she was getting too old… that the opportunity had passed," recalled Ashley when reflecting on the period just before Dora started the school.

As she planned to leave for China, Dora enrolled her daughters in boarding school. Starting a rural school would not be cheap and she would need funds. Because very little is produced in Zambia, almost all products come from other countries, which makes them expensive due to transport and tariff costs. Dora believed that working a higher paying job and raising donations was the fastest pathway to her goal. Justifying this period away from Zambia as a step forward, Dora planned for it to be her last hiatus from the more meaningful work that fueled her. During this time, she also created a YouTube channel and for the first time began sharing her life online. In June 2019 she posted a video clarifying why she was moving. "In a year or two or three... I could have the money to start a school," Dora tells the camera after speaking briefly about the fact that the villages she has worked in need "development not relief." She looks hopeful in the video, but doubt had already begun to creep in. Knowing that she ultimately decided not to move to China, it was hard not to wonder if this video was a last-ditch effort to quell the feeling that she shouldn't leave. She was shouting out her dreams into the universe and hearing nothing in return. Conversations with Dora had made it clear she felt largely unseen or heard as a child and young adult. The internet was a place her voice could be shared. Regardless of who listened, Dora was putting her dream out there. It was this ability to believe in herself and others that she would rely on so heavily in the future. While in front of the camera that day, she didn't have a location for the said school or little more than just a belief that it was possible.

"Yes, I'm very proud of Dora," Mushanga said to me, smiling. He looked past my left shoulder at Dora who reclined against the stiff wooden couch. Speaking in a loud, almost syncopated English, Mushanga told me about his life all the way until Dora appeared. He was born just after independence in 1966 in the Eastern Province, one of four other boys and a single sister. His family worked as subsistence farmers. Eventually his older brother found work in the north part of the Central Province. Jobs being scarce at the time, he sent word to Mushanga, who joined him shortly after. Now some forty years later he was still in that same village, Mapapa. Mushanga had learned English during his limited schooling and while working with others. Thandiwe jumped in to translate when our English conversation began to falter. He then began to tell me when Dora and Alina had first visited together in 2019.

Alina was a teacher herself. She and Dora first met in 2016 at a rural school Dora was visiting in Kapiri. While at the school, Dora worked as a volunteer and met the full-time paid staff,

Alina being one of them. The two became close, sharing a passion for education and an understanding of the development many communities in Zambia desperately needed. Years later, the two remained friends. With Dora's upcoming departure to China, Alina reached out, inviting her to experience village life before leaving. Alina was returning to see her family in the village where she had been raised. Dora had visited many villages and rural schools during her time as a missionary and volunteer teacher. Later, she admitted those experiences were quite different. "I was always a degree removed during previous trips to rural areas. It was like we were 'helping' but never really part of the community. It had a very different feel," Dora said while critically reflecting on some of her earlier work. At the time, she had been doing her best to provide meaningful change, but still she felt it was falling short.

The two women arrived in Mapapa with some simple gifts for the Mushanga family. "The first day when we got to their house we were treated like guests. We ate and talked with the family and then after that day we had chores and were just like everyone else." Dora slept on the floor and when she woke in the morning she would sweep the yard before helping prepare meals. During the afternoon Alina and Dora went on walks through the village. "I was confused because there were all these young children running around and it was the middle of the week. They should've been in school." That evening Dora continued mulling over the reasons why the children were not in school. During her stay, she began to ask further questions. Where was the nearest school? Did villagers drink only from open pit wells? What was the literacy rate among villagers? No one seemed to have the answers. "It became clear that a lot of these children were malnourished or neglected. The girls specifically were at a high risk of being forced into early marriages… the situation was really bad."

Mushanga's wife entered the room; she had not yet spoken to us or offered an introduction. She took a seat on the floor behind his chair and briefly whispered something to him. Rising, she returned outside to the brazier to continue cooking. Mushanga relayed to us that we would be eating shortly, chicken not duck this evening. Having eaten a meal only three hours earlier, a wave of relief washed over me. Even with my extensive travels, I remain a somewhat finicky eater. Knowing the importance of sharing a meal, however, always trumped my proclivity to only eat certain foods. Whatever was served at the Mushanga home was to be eaten in full. Hearing that salty fried chicken was on its way put a broad smile across my face as my stomach relaxed. Mushanga spoke about the Dora he first met years earlier. He described her as humble and determined. Dora, who had also stepped out of the room, returned carrying a large metal platter of food. The four of us washed our hands, using a plastic jug and a small bucket to catch the water as it cascaded off our hands. As we ate, I took in the space around us. The doorway across from me led to the bedroom Dora and Alina shared during their visit. The two had slept on the ground, just as their neighbors did. I wondered what her thoughts were as she stared up at the tin roof, contemplating moving her entire family and life to this desolate little patch of earth. The family cat brushed past my leg. Dora had knowingly chosen a life almost everyone dreamed of escaping; she had willingly joined the ranks of the poor single mothers of the village. There was no glamor or honor in it, which was exactly why it was attractive to her. It was a pure vision of development from within the community.

"I knew in my heart that going to China was not the right decision for me," she later recalled. As she left Mapapa, Dora felt that she had found a meaningful place to start a school. The community desperately needed development. This shift wasn't something she declared on YouTube or to friends and family. It was a personal choice that she needed to consider before diving in fully. "I felt like the decision needed to be all in. I had a lot to consider because I had a job lined up and a lot of people had helped to get me to that point."

That evening as we walked out of Mushanga's house, the

sun had just dipped below the horizon. Families were gathered around their cooking braziers awaiting dinner as the three of us climbed into the car. Deciding to move to Mapapa and start a school came with enormous uncertainties. On her very first visit to this rural part of the nation, Dora had made a decision to become part of this community. The only uncertainty was whether the villagers would let her.

Chapter 8

Mornings at Footprints of Hope began early for everyone. Having rarely slept well, the sound of the rats waking me intermittently, rising early came naturally. Like clockwork, every morning at 6:30, Aunty Prudence would knock on my door with a bucket of boiling water. We would exchange brief "Good mornings," which exhausted most of our linguistic skills at that hour. The Nyambe family dog came along with Aunty Prudence to receive some morning affirmation in the form of a belly rub. Taking the water back to the bathroom, I would begin to mix it with the cold water that had been stored in buckets the night before. Once the temperature was tolerable, I would strip down and begin pouring the water over my head with a third empty bucket. As the water in my reserve bucket cooled, I would add more and more boiling water. All the while a showerhead protruded from the wall directly in front of me.

A few buildings, including the one I stayed in, had plumbing. The school, however, lacked electricity so the only time the toilets flushed and showers ran was when the diesel generator was turned on. During the hottest months of the year Dora would fire up the costly generator and let the kids take cold showers in the afternoon. The school was not glamorous. It didn't have any of the bells and whistles that you might assume based on Dora's massive online audience of over 3.5 million. With that said, it was also impossible to complain on behalf of myself or any of the students. I looked around and felt the gravity of the vulnerable people being helped. To bring up that I had to brush rat poop off my bed in the evening or take a cold bath seemed an affront. The students came from situations that they had in many ways "escaped" for the time being. But the school was more than just a respite; it was a loving and safe home.

Some mornings I spent sitting around a brazier with the young boys. We would stumble through basic English conversations as their bathing water heated up. Like any outsider, I was underwhelmed by their inability to hold even simple conversations in English. I found it hard to understand how any class was held in only English, yet they couldn't answer my basic questions. Reading comprehension would be difficult if telling someone what your favorite color was proved a complex concept. Thoughts like this were quelled the more I came to understand the children sitting around me and the various places they came from. The luckiest few had attended the school since it began only two and a half years earlier. Most had only been enrolled for a relatively short period of time. They spoke solely Bemba at home and in their public lives. The education provided at the school was to a large extent a language immersion experience as much as it was a normal academic institution.

Bemba is a Bantu language along with approximately 440 others. The distinction between language and dialect is hard to define, as many scholars disagree on the extent to which a language must vary for it to be characterized as such. Dora grew up speaking Nyanja, which is "mutually intelligible" (as academics refer to it) to someone who speaks Bemba.[12] This does not mean that the languages are interchangeable or even that speakers of one language can seamlessly transition to the next. It does, however, mean the languages are closely related. It would be more accurate to depict their relationship closer to dialects, albeit this too is an imperfect characterization. As Dora prepared to move to Mapapa, one of her first tasks

---

[12] Bantu Languages, in the *Encyclopedia of Language and Linguistics*, Derek Nurse 2006

was learning the language to a point of local fluency. It was an achievable first step, but nonetheless one of her first obvious hurdles. The others were waiting to present themselves.

As I reflected on her decision to forgo the teaching job in China and move to Mapapa, the number of unknowns seemed almost incomprehensible. Officially making the decision to rescind her earlier decision and move to a rural area to teach created a rift in many of her relationships. From an organizational point of view, Dora had completed her obligations to her previous mission work and left on solid footing. Socially, however, the tight-knit group had a hard time understanding her need to distance herself and start her own project. Dora, however, had her own reason for leaving: an uncompromising vision. She dreamed of a school dedicated to feeding, housing, and educating the most vulnerable members of a rural community. Now free from her organizational responsibilities, Dora was eager to focus solely on development and education. She had a lofty vision for the impact she wanted to have, and although this was certainly intimidating and at times even overwhelming, she couldn't overthink it. Dora dove in headfirst. Securing land, a house, and students were her first priorities.

"Dora came to live with us for a few weeks before she could settle," Mushanga told me while sipping water from his glass. Dora's bridge to Mapapa was this family who had first welcomed her to the area a month earlier. The Mushangas housed Dora and her two oldest daughters. In return, Dora bought food and helped the girls run the household. While staying at the Mushangas, Dora focused on another hurdle to her project—buying a piece of land where she could build a small house and someday a classroom. "At the time my dream was to have a one-room classroom. Sort of like *Little House on the Prairie*. I thought it was something I could probably accomplish and if I could teach and feed the kids in a small school that was good enough for me," she told me.

What she lacked in funding and written plans Dora made up for with mental fortitude and undivided dedication. Dora explained her overview of the problems she assessed when moving to Mapapa. "I looked at everything through this equation of Problem Solution Benefit. What is the problem you are trying to solve, what is your current solution for that problem, and how will that benefit the people you are trying to help." This was a vast oversimplification of the enormous task at hand, but its simplicity is what helped Dora focus on only the essential nature of her goal. The most basic problem was lack of water, food, and education among the village children. The benefit was water, food, education, and stability. The solution was being worked out each day as she learned more about the community she was dedicating herself to.

The purchase and ownership of land in Zambia, especially in rural areas, is more complicated than simply finding a plot and buying it from the previous owner. All land in Zambia is overseen by tribal chiefs. Each chief rules over a specific portion of the country and all the land that falls within that area is theirs. This ownership of land allows the chief to both rent and sell land to villagers. There are two ways in which land can be sold. A villager can buy land from the chief and then sell it to other villagers. This land, regardless of how many times it exchanges hands, remains under the ownership of the chief.[13] In a sense, when the villager initially buys the land they are purchasing an indefinite lease on the land. The only way to truly "own" the land and distance oneself from the chief is to "liberate" the land. This is an expensive and lengthy process that requires approval by the chief who can, at any point, deny the request. It is a system I found hard to understand as it clearly benefits the farming corporations with more capital and hurts small local landowners. The downside of owning "unliberated land" is that the owner is subject to the rulings of the local tribal chief. Staying in his good graces requires gifts, perhaps more accurately, bribes. When I first was being taught this system, I asked why the president didn't step in

[13] A perspective on indigenous land tenure systems and land concentration. In R.E. Downs & S.P. Reyna (eds.),Bruce, J. W. (1988). Land and Society in Contemporary Africa. Hanover, NH: University Press of New England.

to make changes. They laughed, amused at my naivete. "He's the biggest chief of them all." The landscape of operating any organization in Zambia was becoming clearer. There wasn't just corruption to worry about but also a legal system not set up to accelerate success.

"I took Dora to the headman and she told him her plan and then also shared it with others in the village," Mushanga told me. On the car ride home, Dora informed me that during those meetings she was largely thought to be an idiot and dismissed as an outsider and unable to accomplish anything because she was a woman. Even with this initial pushback, Mushanga was able to find her a plot of land about a twenty-minute walk from Mapapa. Stepping foot on the virgin land, Dora looked around and admired the many tall trees and the wide, open field behind the property. She sank almost all her savings into the land. She was now committed both to Mapapa and her dream of starting a school there.

"The land was on an old graveyard and many people feared that place," Mushanga said.

"And you?" I asked. "How did you feel about the land?"

"Me, I am not afraid. That is why I was encouraging her to buy the land. There were some people saying and doing strange things, but it was good land."

At the time of purchase Dora was unaware that in the corner

of her property was a small, unmarked graveyard. "Even if I would have known, I still would have bought the land. It was a good location and plot. I also didn't have much money so it was the best option."

Dora now had the right to build a house and begin her project. Still under the purview of the chief, she had yet to meet him and establish their relationship. Still sleeping on Mushanga's floor, Dora began to plan how she would build a house. Out of money and with mounting internal pressure to launch her project, Dora decided the girls and she would build and live in a mud hut. It was a temporary solution, she told them, saying that a burnt brick house would be erected once things became a bit more stable. Hearing this retelling, "stable" struck me as an odd word to describe the settling-in period to a mud house. Dora's focus was always looking forward. She felt "busy" trying to get her life in order just enough so that she could start lessons. Building a physical classroom was still a dream far off. Using the last of her funds, she bought five bags of cement. A woman from the village advised Dora on the best way to build her mud home and they promptly began construction. The cement was used for the flooring and provided a clean base to work from. When completed, the one-room hut was approximately seven-by-seven feet with the roof just above the tops of their heads.

"I was deeply concerned," Ashley said about Dora's decision to move into the mud house. Dora was a twenty-seven-year-old single mother. Her two daughters, ages fifteen and seventeen, were not far behind and perhaps had little idea of the risk to their own safety. Dora had witnessed success and completion of goals within other organizations, but she had never been at the beginning of any of those missions. She had not witnessed the planning from vision to reality. Many of the organizations and people she had worked with were very experienced; they had a team, funding, and not only goals but also plans of how to achieve those goals. Dora's vision of starting a school would have been at the top of the outline for these organizations, followed by pages of steps to make that happen. Dora certainly had no outline, and her plan was simply to start.

"About a month after Dora arrived she shifted to the mud hut. I knew she would work hard to help the village. I wasn't sure what exactly that would look like," Mushanga said as I scooped the last of the rice and relish combination into my mouth. From the outside, this period was perhaps the most uncertain in her journey. Dora, however, saw this step as an accomplishment rather than a grim reminder of how much farther was left. Now independent and on their own, the young woman could begin her school.

Speaking with Dora about this stage, her single-minded

vision impressed me. "It was hard to move here," she said. "I knew that people needed development and it kept me going." At the time Dora didn't have low expectations of what she would accomplish. Rather, she saw every inch forward as a step in the right direction.

Dora certainly did not lack optimism, but any outside organization would have openly doubted her realism. She had no corporate backing or institutional funding. There was no plan to secure funding through any government program or religious group. Comparative NGOs in Zambia have well-drawn-out plans often with very specific goals. Most NGOs, such as Aids Health Foundation, OxFam, and WaterAid, have distinct mission statements that help them focus their mission as well as focus on potential donors. Of course, there is not an unlimited supply of aid money, and this means that establishing an organization as legitimate is essential to an NGO's existence. Footprints of Hope had a vision, but no plan on how to fund the education and nutrition of the children it hoped to improve.

Many villagers saw Dora as an outsider, dangerous to their way of life and something to get rid of. In part this was true. Dora was an outsider; she had grown up in Zambia's metropolitan centers. Though she was not above raising her own chickens, boiling her water, and tending a garden, it was not ingrained in her. Further, Dora was unwilling to yield to men. To them she was a radical feminist, a woman with adopted children who had the gall to come in and attempt to create change. "Change is a scary thing to many of these people. Even if it can help them, a lot of people feel threatened," she said to me. These threats began to escalate from dismissal of her and her goals to outright intimidation.

Buying land that contained a small graveyard further fueled the rumors. After moving into the mud hut, strange things began to happen. "I would wake up and see one-legged dog footprints around the hut. There would be 'charms' placed around the property. They were really trying to intimidate me." Witchcraft has deep cultural roots in Zambia; it is not uncommon to read newspaper headlines such as "Kasenengwa boy (17) dies after eating love portion" (Published in July of 2022, "Potion" spelled incorrectly, appearing on the front page of the *Zambia Daily Mail*).[14] There were also many more sinister reasons to practice supposed witchcraft. Driving along the roads, whether in the capital or in small rural towns, large signs for witch doctors can be seen offering myriad services. It mattered little that Dora didn't believe in witchcraft; it was the intimidation and trespassing that worried her. "We had

---

[14] 17 Year Old Dies After Taking Love Portion, Zambia Daily Mail, Mayengo Nyirenda, July 7, 2022

a very real conversation about how fast Dora could unlock the padlocks on her door and escape if someone set her roof on fire," Ashley told me, remembering the worries she held for her friend.

Alcoholism is a big problem in rural areas of Zambia. It was a distinct possibility that a jaded drunk would attempt to burn down Dora's home. Inside a mud thatched house, she would have only a few moments to escape before the roof collapsed and it was too late. The house had no windows, which perhaps kept them safer in some ways, but it also increased the risk that if a fire ever started, their lives would quickly be in jeopardy. When we spoke about these concerns, Dora was measured, but the pain broke through in her voice when she remembered some of the darkest moments. Both in her childhood and adult life there had been an overwhelming number of negative voices beating her down. In more ways than before, these voices had grown in magnitude and taken on a more physical presence.

Though I knew she had overcome many of these insecurities, it was clear Dora still felt slighted by many of the villagers. She showed a level of grace with them that I've seen in few others. Her goal to bring development to the village trumped any of the ill will that lingered. When we spoke about her early years and the negative impact of friends, family, and those around her, the hurt remained. Dora wasn't trying to prove herself to anyone by starting the school, but she did still hold many of these hurtful things close to her, and it impacted to a great deal her self-perception.

Days after moving in, Dora began to send word to the villagers that she would be teaching classes. Her first lesson was taught under a tall mpundu tree that arched overhead providing ample shade. "I wasn't sure anyone would even show up, so I made popcorn and sort of lured them in with the promise of food," Dora said, laughing. The first day a handful of kids showed up for a free snack and some English lessons. Footprints of Hope was born. The focus of the school in those early stages was equally to educate and to check on the children's overall welfare. Still new to the area and still becoming integrated in the community, Dora was learning more about the problems the children faced. Serving popcorn and providing a safe space for the kids was as important as anything they learned in class during those early days.

Sitting in the cinder block building that is now the school of Footprints of Hope, with its strong walls and polished tile floor, it is somewhat unbelievable to hear about a time when Dora was living in a mud hut nearby. An afternoon breeze swept through the open windows, making the paper chains hanging from the exposed rafters rustle. Dora told me about the many nights her daughters would cry and how scared the three of them were at times. I had seen her YouTube videos from this period, and even her upbeat narration could not hide the fact that they were struggling. It felt almost voyeuristic to watch her second-eldest daughter cook and eat a rat she had killed. Dora talked optimistically about the future of Footprints of Hope, the name she had given her project. The videos give a glimpse into their home, which Dora would refer to me less than affectionately as "the shack." At times she was candid with the camera about the difficulty of life in the bush. Her videos about getting water from an open pit well struck the viewer with the realities of her life.

It was hard to imagine a foreigner having any real empathy for the struggle she and the villagers were going through. How could Dora communicate the impact of forced marriages, malnutrition, water insecurity, and the pervasive poverty mindset? Together I sat with Dora while she traced images for the children's English lesson the following day. When we walked through periods of time in her life, it felt almost as if it was the first time she appreciated the depth of what she had accomplished. Dora knew she had a strength that others often underestimate, but as I sat across from her, mouth wide open, asking, "How? Why? What made you think you could possibly figure this out?" she seemed to come to the same realization as I.

Chapter 9

Like the bush fires that spread in the tall dry grass through-out the rural Zambian countryside, word of Dora's school spread. Villagers spoke to one another about the single mother living in a hut teaching classes and feeding children. During those first weeks, Dora and her daughters would wake up and remove everything from the hut. Then they would work on sweeping it out and cleaning the dust from their belongings. The home, with wide gaps between the roof and walls, was constantly invaded by insects and small rodents. The three worked independently on household and school jobs during the early afternoon to ensure things ran smoothly. "Veronica and Grace were an incredible help. I couldn't have done it without my daughters," Dora said.

As the school slowly began to attract students, Dora started to assess the development needs of her new community. Between six to twelve students would arrive around ten in the morning for their daily lesson while sitting in a semicircle under the broad mpundu tree. Dora would work through a small core curriculum. Often the children would laugh at her mispronunciation of Bemba words and try to correct her. Still in her infancy with the new language, she often misspoke. "When I was first learning I would accidentally offend people sometimes because I would try to say one thing but it would come across differently." Most people took this in stride, working with Dora to help her Bemba skills improve. Without a vehicle Dora was reliant on bush taxis. These old run-down beasts crawled from village to village until they reached the nearest city and were easily identifiable with usually a few live chickens tied to the roof and packed with five to seven people over capacity. Dora was intimately acquainted with all modes of transport from the school to the small town of Masansa where she bought food and supplies; the town was also her nearest point of social interaction.

The sun was beginning to set as Dora and I walked down the dusty village road along with her dog, Anna. Villagers passed by as they returned from the farm blocs and local market after a day of work. Dora slowed as we approached a small footpath to our right. Turning, we walked a few paces until we arrived at one of the first boreholes she had installed for the village. It was the only one I had not yet visited. During my time in the village the boreholes had transformed from instruments of utility into tangible monuments to Dora's work here. They were unimpressive in size and possessed no artistic or visually pleasing elements, yet they reflected a dream she once had. I was unsure what Dora saw when she looked at them—likely just a source of water. The physical nature of the boreholes became tangible objects for me to utilize in understanding the impact Dora first had in this remote corner of Zambia. She was a woman with little to no financial means who had managed to pull clean water from this barren patch of earth. It was her incredible effort and focus on inducing positive change, regardless of the opinions of others, that makes her unique. Dora herself is most proud of the intangible changes she is making in her community, yet these silver fountains now scattered throughout her community are prominent reminders of her broad impact on all members of her community.

The cultural changes and increased access to quality education are ongoing work that Dora recognizes as unlikely to ever be "finished" or "accomplished." When Dora first started teaching, the villagers had grown increasingly wary the longer she remained. In Masansa, a fast-developing farming hub of sorts, she was just any other Zambian. Back in the village, she was a threat to the traditional livelihood and the culture of those around her. When Dora initially moved into the mud hut, she hired a local man to stand watch at the front of the property each night. This quelled some of her concerns, but as he was unarmed it was unlikely he could provide protection in the face of a legitimate threat. "We were so concerned we actually gave her our dog," Ashley told me, almost laughing as she remembered the worry she had for her friend. Ashley told me that she still has concerns regarding Dora's safety, but her confidence in Dora's situation has grown dramatically. Although the Nyambe home was not far from the road, their relative isolation was not to be underestimated. If an emergency occurred there wasn't cell service strong enough to even call for help. Emergency services, such as patrol cars and ambulances, don't exist in the same capacity in Mapapa as in other parts of Zambia.

Rather than focus on the increasing tension she was creating, Dora poured her energy into her students. She worked with them on basic English and math skills, all the while trying to entice others to attend class. Concurrently, a small donation was sent from friends Dora had worked with over the previous years. Grateful for the donation but unable to afford much, Dora took the entirety of it and built an oven to fire bricks of her own. The hut she and the girls lived in had become seriously infested with termites, and despite spraying with insecticide and cleaning daily, it looked as though they would have to move out soon. The oven allowed them to create enough bricks for a small classroom and modest home. Dora, more focused on the school, chose to build the classroom first.

Creating mud burnt bricks is a laborious process that Dora and her two daughters threw themselves into. A few villagers, aware of Dora's mission and supportive of her, showed up intermittently to help. Through her growing acquaintances, the rumors that had been circulated were finally being shared with Dora. Claims that Dora was a satanist were the most shared among the villagers and many wholeheartedly believed them. One woman launched a vicious series of allegations accusing Dora of using the village and children for her own personal gain. Eventually the woman showed up at Dora's home and confronted her. Calmly, Dora left her property and went to the Masansa police to report the issue and threatened to prosecute her on various charges. The outright harassment from this villager came to an end after Dora's quick action.

The most hurtful allegations were in relation to Dora's supposed satanic worship. Witchcraft and "African magic," as Mushanga told me, have deep cultural roots in this part of Zambia and as such, accusations can cause real repercussions.

Over the previous five years, Dora's life had been dedicated to mission work, education, and development. She had given up employment opportunities that were rarely available to Zambian women to move to Mapapa. The time and energy people put into circulating these rumors about practicing witchcraft was an affront to her sacrifice.

As a young person, Dora was largely involved in the Christian community. She attended faith-based schools and worked for a Christian mission organization. Faith still played a role in her personal life but was no longer a driving force. While working for the missionary organizations on development efforts Dora recalled the villagers being very receptive to outside help. This is perhaps, in part, because she had never stayed long enough to see what was needed in the next step of the mission. The transition from relief work into a role of a community leader was not seamless. Creating lasting development was necessary, but the roadmap to do so was unclear. "When I moved here, I came with a relief mindset... I thought I was going to show up and save them from poverty or this mindset that they had." Specifically, their complacency toward malnutrition and child marriages. Seeing young girls being the subject of abuse was something Dora felt personally compelled to change. Her work with young Dalit woman and her own trauma gave her unique empathy for these young villagers.

After returning from our visit to the borehole, I joined Dora in her kitchen. As I sat at the small wooden table with my notebook open, she stood across the table from me, chopping carrots. Nandi peeked in and said, "Hi Mommy," her voice rising as she elongated the "e" sound. Seeing Nandi intermittently since her arrival, I watched as she found her footing in her new family and in school. Dora was doing everything in her power to help her and it seemed to be working. Nandi seemed happy and more confident. She had gained necessary weight and was no longer as frail as when I met her. Every subsequent visit after first meeting her, she continued to look stronger and healthier. Personally, I felt attached to her journey and it pained me to know how much further she had to go. Seeing me that evening, she smiled and addressed me. "Hi Uncle Joe." Her slight speech impediment concerned Dora but remained far down on the list of priorities for bolstering the young girl's future. Nandi still needed surgery to remove the genital warts she had contracted. It would be a painful and emotional experience. Dora knew that it was important to first strengthen her physically and emotionally before the necessary medical procedure.

Seeing Dora interact with her children reminded me that the mother of twelve standing at the table was still only twenty-nine.

Dora shared the same traits as many of her twenty-year-old contemporaries. While she cooked that afternoon, music played from the patio, and when a favorite song came on Dora sang and danced. Her favorite songs I categorized in my notebook as "girl boss" songs. Meghan Trainor, Beyonce, and Disney princesses were some of the stylings that unleashed this side of Dora. On Tuesdays and Thursdays, the school would gather in the cafeteria after dinner and have a dance party. The entire school would dance and sing their hearts out for over an hour. Seeing Dora lead choreographed dances and freestyle to her heart's content reminded me of our proximity in age and that she was still very young.

During those nights of dancing in the cafeteria, breaks needed to be taken to allow the students to cool down. In these short intermissions the older boys would grab buckets of water to pour on the ground to limit the amount of dust kicked up and subsequently inhaled. I looked around during those evenings at the children and teachers and saw legs dotted with mud from the wet sandy floor. This connected me to the deeper meaning of what was happening at the school. Many of the students surrounding me had been through more trauma than I could fathom. Yet for that hour, we would dance, sweat, and sing seemingly without a care in the world. In those moments, I felt more emotionally connected to the students and their dreams than at any other time. As I gasped for air and they laughed at my awkward movements, I met them on common ground.

While we talked about the community's pushback, Dora finished chopping the carrots and continued to prepare dinner. She was critical of her own actions early on. "I had the whole white savior complex. I had the whole savior, not the white... like, I have come to liberate you and to guide you to freedom. Which is known as education. What I didn't see was that I would have some resistance from people. So that was a very big shock to me." It was a difficult lesson for her to learn. Forced to step back and reflect on the perception of the villagers, Dora took a different approach. "This was real," she said, reflecting on the initial months of establishing the school. "I had moved my family and there was no backing out. It was a big moment... I needed to learn how to use their knowledge and incorporate their culture into what I was trying to do." Dora's humility despite the outright attacks on her changed the dynamic of her mission.

Three years ago, instead of being the village teacher, Dora became a student again. She looked to others for guidance on where to build and how to understand the land and culture of the rural community. "I was from 'town' and people saw me as different. Parts of the culture were backwards," Dora said, referring to the sexual misconduct, early marriages, and certain child-rearing practices. "But what I needed to focus on was that they have ancestral knowledge and I could learn from that." Dora had learned a great deal from interacting with people from around the globe. It took a concerted effort for her to ignore those feelings and step back to see the bigger picture. To make progress in Mapapa, Dora needed to become a part of the community before she could convince anyone that progress and development would be beneficial. That process took time, and while she continued learning and building the school, rumors continued to spread. A father and the chief's secretary, Grant Chibuye, participated in spreading the rumors directly to the chief himself. On a sunny morning while I was writing in the empty dining hall, one of the older boys came running in to summon me to the library. Taking my shoes off before entering (as all the children did), I greeted the seven adults seated on two couches. Dora sat directly across the room from an older couple. Chibuye sat to my left and Dora quickly introduced us. The meeting was to finalize the purchase of additional land that Dora hoped to build a village clinic on. The couple was there to receive the final payment and Chibuye was a chiefdom witness of sorts. Dressed in slacks, a faded red dress shirt, a tracksuit jacket, and a black bucket hat, his appearance was rather jocular. After the meeting, Chibuye spoke to me about the school. I learned his first daughter, who was likely in her forties, was employed to clean the school. Chibuye's youngest daughter was a seventh-year student whom I knew quite well. Chibuye himself was seventy-seven years old. His grandson was also enrolled in the school and his niece was one of the teachers. He spoke highly about the school and Dora, inferring as a member of the PTO that he also helped the community and school make great strides. Shortly after leaving I would come to learn that at first he was adamantly against Dora. Most likely he was threatened by this young, educated woman who possessed skills and abilities far greater than his own. Regardless of his reasons, it was ironic to hear praise and self-congratulation from a man who had, like so many others, had spread ill will.

After leaving the library that morning, we crossed over the eroded mound that Dora's mud hut once sat atop. Pausing, I asked her what it was like to live in the hut, isolated and unsure of the future. The lunch bell was struck and the kids ran past us to the dining hall. My question was swallowed up. Turning to me, Dora said, "Starting to feed the kids lunch everyday was a big milestone. I still wasn't eating correctly because it was hard to get certain things." While in the process of building the classroom and slightly larger brick home, Dora began to offer free lunches to her students. The meals were basic but provided nutrition to students who likely were getting one meal a day at home. Dora was quick to recognize the struggle many of the villagers were in yet seemed to ignore the precarious balance she maintained during this time. She was a self-defined picky eater as a child, and this had largely carried over into adulthood. Dora avoided certain carbs and although she ate traditional Zambian food was not as taken by nshima as her peers. She told me that while living in the hut they got sick all the time with rashes and allergies and constant stomach pains. These ailments were the likely result of the water the women were consuming. "The open pit well had frogs, insects, and oftentimes we would have to fish out small dead animals that fell in." Drinking bottled water and being increasingly wary of the well water helped alleviate some of these issues, but their overall health continued to suffer. It was during this time that Dora's first goal of development materialized.

In order to educate the children in her community, Dora would also need to attend to their greater well-being. Initially, she had enticed children to attend her lessons with snacks; at this stage she was feeding them a basic but nutritious lunch. The water that was a detriment to her own health was no doubt affecting the lives of everyone in the village. Drilling a borehole and providing the community with clean water was a tangible goal. As Dora began to think about how to raise the money for such a project, she continued to share inconsistent video updates on YouTube. The growth of her online presence was stagnant, and she had no clear path to raising the money needed to dig a borehole. Most NGOs would never have been in that position. They would have planned financially for whatever projects they would take on, or they would be more realistic and accept their organization's limitations. Instead of focusing on the enormous challenge that she faced, Dora continued teaching and bringing in more students from the village. She worked on meeting parents and members of the community to dispel the myths they had learned about her.

Dora's daughters were often less than thrilled with their new life in the village. They were thankful for their mother's support and love but found themselves bored and far from the cities they once knew. Dora told me that, "Grace was very bored one afternoon and wanted me to download TikTok and I thought it could be fun so I went ahead and got the app." When Ashley and I talked about this seemingly innocuous decision, she wondered whether it was a way to alleviate the loneliness Dora felt. Removed from her previous life filled with work colleagues and friends, Dora was on an island of sorts. Social media was a way, if only virtually, to become connected with others. Posting her first video as "DoraMoonoNyambe," she launched herself into a virtual community that would become an integral part of her journey.

Chapter 10

As I limped my Toyota Hilux back to my apartment in Livingstone, I recorded a short clip of myself recounting the previous days. After camping for over a week in the remote Western Province of Zambia, I had blown my radiator in the bush. Conducting ecotourism research in a remote area was incredible in many ways but also a crash course on auto mechanics. For two days Samuel (my research assistant and Wildlife Police officer) and I waited until a tractor was finally able to reach us and drag us out. Despite worries about totaling my car, I was able to cobble the radiator together and drive the twelve hours home overnight. Arriving in Livingstone, my face was covered in dust and oil from the previous days. That night I opened TikTok and watched as Dora shared a short clip of her life. TikTok was designed and largely marketed as a kids' dance app. However, like many tools, TikTok has multiple uses and the woman on my screen had co-opted the application as a window into her new life's mission. She shared the ups and downs of being a single adoptive mother, the director of an NGO, and a teacher. As I scrolled down, I watched people around the world react to cat videos, visit new places, and speak about their passions in life. TikTok has a lighthearted nature and since its inception few people have taken it seriously as a challenger to the likes of Instagram and Facebook. Many young people, however, saw it in a different light. I too had come to appreciate TikTok as a tool to share less edited real-life moments from each day.

As an application, the most prominent feature that attracts new users is the FYP (For You Page). The FYP is without a doubt the reason TikTok was the most downloaded app in the world in both 2020 and 2021. The FYP, which is the initial user landing page, uses an intuitive algorithm to source new videos that meet your specific viewing behavior. The app follows your every move as you scroll through each full screen video. If you like or comment on a video of an a cappella singer, rest assured you will be seeing more of that in the future. The app doesn't just take into account the inputs that you give it but also the amount of time you spend before scrolling and the videos you share and save. It's both incredible and unnerving how well the algorithm learns your patterns. For many users, the unnerving part is realizing the app understands both your conscious and subconscious tendencies and then uses them to keep you scrolling. The algorithm is a powerful tool that has enabled fully unknown creators to be launched into internet stardom seemingly overnight. Unlike Facebook, Instagram, or Twitter where the main way to connect and consume content is by searching and finding it yourself, TikTok uses this algorithm to source videos that fit your brand of entertainment.

Authenticity is a word that is often thrown around when talking about social media and the effect it has on our world view. As both a consumer and a creator, I first began to experience this when I downloaded the app just before moving to Zambia. TikTok has built-in features to enhance your facial structure, whiten your teeth, and add cute freckles to your face. I have no doubt the effects of these and other elements of the platform will be judged harshly when young people grow up and look back. Yet it's the same app that is host to some of the most honest conversations. It's a microcosm of funny, sad, exciting, and vulnerable moments of normal humans just reaching out into the void of the internet and sharing their life. It was for that reason I felt compelled to download the app just prior to arriving in Zambia as a Fulbright Scholar.

Like most people, Dora's inaugural video on the platform was about as unremarkable as you'd imagine. Using the front-facing camera and a filter that superimposed sunglasses on her face, a song plays and then her daughter Grace pops into view and begins dancing. It's a relatable video but did little to launch Dora into the "influencer" status she could now lay claim to if she chose. Talking to Dora about titles such as "influencer" or "social media celebrity" always made us both laugh. During my first visit to the school and while waiting at the hospital a woman approached Dora and me. Cocking her head she looked at us and said, "Don't I know you from TikTok?" I laughed and leaned back, allowing the woman to see Dora more clearly. "No," she said, "You. You're Joe, right?" Dora and I looked at each other and both let out a laugh. There we were at a remote village health post and there was a Zambian woman who somehow knew me, this tiny creator with a few followers, while I'm sitting next to the "village TikToker" as Dora often refers to herself. By the time I met Dora she had gained over 3.4 million followers on TikTok and was consistently creating viral content.

Whether her journey on TikTok began out of boredom, loneliness, or the desire to share her life's work is hard to decipher, but once she first started posting Dora didn't stop. Watching and discussing her initial posts on the app, it was clear she was feeling out what this new platform was capable of. On her tenth post she shared a video of herself lip-syncing "Broken and Beautiful" by Kelly Clarkson. Superimposing an explanation of her age and her adoption journey she clicked post in May of 2020. The video went viral and now, two years later, that initial post that helped garner her the first wave of global attention has over seven million views. When we spoke about that first wave of followers, Dora recalled that she was overwhelmed that people were taking such an interest in her. Despite the attention on the social media site, Dora didn't begin to translate it into anything more than a fun or active social media presence.

The heat of the summer was returning while I was visiting the school in August of 2022. I wandered over to the football pitch and sat atop the small hill near the gate of the school. Notebook in hand, I began to reflect on the conversation Dora and I had earlier that morning. Our talks were always a combination of her airing the duties and stress of the present and me probing about the past. Now under the glaring sun, I sat alone in one of the places Dora could often be found loitering. This hill was coincidentally one of the best places to get cell reception. There are videos of her waiting in agony, her phone raised to the sky while she tried to upload a video or post a photo. I enjoyed sitting on the hill and watching the kids play on the football field at its base. They would show off their skills and call for my attention, always looking for words of affirmation and high fives. Spending time with the students in this way always felt productive, even though I rarely wrote much. Of all the things Dora and I did together during those months of interviews, being a friend to the students was one of the things I enjoyed the most. Seeing the boys tackle one another and the girls play various games and compliment each other was a constant reminder of why Dora was here. Intangible moments such as these were near impossible to share on social media and Dora rarely tried.

During her first two months of posting consistently, Dora focused on creating short vlog-style videos and updates on everyday life in Mapapa. Each post grew her following steadily and as this happened her confidence also grew. This confidence translated into the realization that her voice was being heard and she had the opportunity to speak directly to people around the world. That evening, sitting under the tin roof that extended off her house, I asked about that early message she was trying to share. "I want the narrative of an African child to change. I don't want when people think of an African child, they think of, oh, uneducated, uncivilized people. I want them to think, okay, fine. Yes, they are from a third-world country. But they have risen above that and they are doing so many amazing things." Dora has a strong presence and is able to speak openly about the issues the school and the community face. Yet I had to wonder how many people watched her content and had their stereotypes confirmed rather than dispelled.

Dora was sharing stories of abuse, malnutrition, and cultural practices such as forced marriage that most foreigners would see as stuck in the past. Being at the school, I could see the impact and the growth of the students, the nuance in each story Dora told and the broader picture. Her goal was to educate and uplift the children of a rural community, and she did that by motivating people from around the world to donate and help her mission. The TikTok algorithm, however, rewarded dramatic stories and the hardships she and students endured. Often her most honest and open videos about the logistics of the school, education, or positive cultural changes were overlooked. It was paradoxical that she was working to help change the legacy of the community, but the content that garnered the most attention often affirmed other negative world views. I asked Dora about the voyeuristic tendency of some of her viewers or even followers. "I think that many people watch my videos and they are not supportive or they see it and think that it represents all of Africa. But that's not fair to me. I only represent Dora. How is it fair that I represent a whole country or continent?" It was a question that we both felt strongly about. After months of watching every piece of content she had ever created, and hours of time spent with her and the students, I knew their journey intimately. Dora didn't represent Zambia, nor did she try to. It was admirable in many ways that she felt her content was designed for an educated viewer. Dora came to TikTok each morning to share her personal vision. She never felt compelled to talk about Zambia as a country or Africa broadly because how could she represent either?

Dora was Zambian by birth but often said she felt most like a third culture kid. This phrase, "third culture" was something I learned only upon moving to Zambia. Third culture kids are simply children of immigrants who don't have a firm cultural identity. Dora's mother, despite spending most of her life in Zambia, was most closely related to South African culture, and Dora's father was completely absent from her life. This meant Dora's cultural identity was a mix, and neither while in South Africa nor Zambia did she ever feel fully seen. At first I found this hard to understand because Dora is likely one of the more famous Zambians in the world at the moment. The more Zambians I met, however, the more I began to understand this feeling. Zambia is a country of many different tribes, ethnicities, races, and religions. Like my home, it is impossible to say what a "normal" American or Zambian experience is or was.

"I know that the supporters I have on TikTok understand that I represent myself only. I share the things that happen to me and the vision I have for our children here. Beyond that it's not fair. I'm just Dora."

Over the first two months of her online presence on TikTok, Dora did just that: She focused on herself. She spoke about who she was, why she had adopted children, and the journey she had already embarked on. In some videos she showed her old mud home, gave brief cooking tutorials, and shared happy moments with her students. Reading the comments section on these videos, I found a mix of curiosity and support. In hindsight, watching these videos, it was obvious that even if she had not realized it yet, the hardest part was over. By the time Dora's follower count had begun to mushroom, she was already living in a semi-stable home. I say semi-stable as it would collapse a few months after moving in. Dora never shared the hardest initial months on TikTok. Other than a few photos and stories about that time, few people understand the enormous hardships she faced when first moving to Mapapa.

As Dora used her charismatic energy and passion to share the journey, followers began to take greater notice of the need not being met in Mapapa. After only three months on the platform, calls from supporters had grown so loud Dora was convinced to set up a GoFundMe page, a crowdsourcing platform that enables supporters to help fund charitable missions or projects they feel connected to. GoFundMe is only supported in nineteen countries, all of which are in Europe or North America. The official website states that if you are outside these countries, "you can always ask a friend who lives in a supported country to start a fundraiser on your behalf." In late May of 2020, Footprints of Hope launched their first GoFundMe campaign. "We set our goal at five thousand dollars and I remember talking to Ashley about it and her telling me it was a high goal. She didn't want to see me let down and we really didn't have any idea how many people would donate."

It was getting late as Dora and I began to wrap up our conversation that evening. The kids in the dining hall would be getting anxious, waiting for their nightly activity to start. I had one last question before we would make the two-minute walk to the center of campus. "Did you ever explore grants, government funding, or support from one single organization either here in Zambia or abroad?" Dora was pensive for a moment. "I never want the Zambian government to be involved. Bringing them into the picture would completely change this place. I've worked so hard from the very first day to establish a culture and environment where the kids are safe and have the best chance for the future. I want to work my absolute hardest to keep that control." After having worked with the Zambian government to gain research clearance, visas, and automotive permits, I understand her aversion. Despite being a peaceful and stable government, Zambia's federal government is bureaucratic and has deeply rooted corruption issues.

I nodded. "Why not involve larger NGOs or charities that could take the pressure of individual funding away?" She pushed her hands parallel to her body and shifted herself back on the chair. "From my experience with the ones that I've dealt with," she began, referring to Mission Organizations and NGOs, "there's always a hierarchy. A person can come from the US, have zero experience in whatever field that is. The fact that they're white, they will have an upper hand in that organization more than me, the person who's on the ground who has done this." As she spoke it was as though I was no longer on the porch. She was not so much answering my question as recalling the lived experience of working for years under management in various organizations. "So in me involving organizations or wanting to partner with an organization, I'm like, I will go back to the same cycle of it being I have the knowledge, I have the skills, I will get used by the person who gets not really the credit, but the person who gets the last word." Her back had straightened and she looked past my shoulder toward the untamed bush beyond the school.

"I honestly didn't want that. And I also didn't want a situation whereby my vision, my goal of how I wanted things to be done, to be questioned by somebody else, because my vision, how I look at things, how I look at the world is my own." Dora broke into a wily smile and looked me dead in the eye and said, "And also I feel like I was not born to work under somebody." We both laughed, understanding she was both speaking something true to herself but also self-deprecating her "I can do it myself" attitude that carried throughout every part of her life. During many of our conversations Dora broke character like this, but what was always funny to me was that the "character" she played was the professional head of NGO; her reality was Dora. She remains a passionate teacher and woman who values kindness over just about everything else.

"No. No, no organizations for me. Sorry. Mhm." Getting up to head over to the dining hall for game night she turned her head toward me and said, "And honestly, I just wanted to prove to everybody else who said I couldn't do it, that really I could." In the first two weeks of the GoFundMe campaign, Dora began to prove the doubters wrong. Translating a NGO's social media presence, specifically a TikTok account, into a monetary venture was uncharted territory not only for Dora but for people across the African continent. For all the talk she has about representing only herself, Dora was and is a pioneer who represents a greater group of young Africans creating grassroots change. Despite her good intentions, the donation page still had to be run through a proxy in the US. Barriers of entry such as this only reinforced others' negative stereotypes of Africans working to help themselves and be the change they wished to see. Despite this and other potential challenges, Dora raised over US$20,000 in the first weeks of the campaign. As the money started to pour in, she was overwhelmed by the support of strangers from around the world. Beyond just financial support, it was the moral support from thousands of people cheering her on that had the biggest impact on her social media presence. At the five-week mark the campaign had raised over US$50,000, smashing her initial goal. For the first time, Dora began to realize the enormous power of the platform.

Chapter 11

The yellow gate swung open and the students on the playground came running toward my blue pickup truck. I was returning to both Footprints of Hope and Zambia after a short absence in Malawi. I had known many of these students now for eight months. Coming back to Zambia felt like returning home, or at least the place I felt most at home since graduating college almost three years earlier. Upon seeing the students, I was immediately reminded of what had drawn me here in the first place. They eagerly shouted out my name and waved. Not a polite one-handed wave, but that gleeful double-arm windshield wiper wave that can't help but make you smile. I greeted many of them back with their own names and was repaid with instant and massive grins. From my very first visit to the school, I made it a personal point of pride to try to learn and interact by name with as many of Dora's students as possible. As a foreigner, being invited into both Dora's life and the school was not something I took lightly. The kids called me "Teacher Joe," a title I didn't feel like I had earned but loved, nonetheless.

Earlier that morning, I had left the capital after a research meeting and was eager to drive north to see the students and teachers. I had been living in Zambia for over seven months and my relationship with the teachers, students, and staff had deepened greatly. In a large part they had become my link to Zambia outside of my research. For many foreigners—both tourists and expats—breaking out of the proverbial bubble never occurs. In part this is perhaps due to their apathy in seeing anything beyond what they envisioned they would see in Zambia. But even those who do wish to break out of this circle find it extremely difficult. Zambian culture varies greatly throughout the country and is far different from most cultures outside of the African continent. Over my entire time in Zambia, I never could say I "understood" or fully grasped the culture. It was a constant lesson in appreciating nuance and small everyday interactions.

After spending time with Dora and being invited into her world, she naturally took on the role of educator with me. She was willing to act as a bridge to difficult and uncomfortable conversations that were vital to help me better understand my place in Zambia. The two of us were able to talk about various topics that would likely not be broached by expats even after living in Zambia for years. I felt honored to have a place to bring these questions. Dora always focused on representing her own lived experience, and this was essential in the formation of my own view of Zambia.

From a larger perspective she was working to do this more broadly with every interaction she had on TikTok. When talking about her ability to connect on an individual level with users of the platform, Dora deferred to her "Problem Solution Benefit" analogy. "In every video I try to say, here's the problem, what was the solution we used, and what is the benefit. This equation is very key. It allows anyone watching to be able to see the impact our community has for these kids." After having watched the entire catalog of Dora's content both on TikTok and other platforms, it was clear to me that she employed this strategy most prominently on TikTok. Dora's ability to connect on an emotional level with her community she whittled down to "Just being genuine, I think. Being authentic and being me. I don't know how to be anybody else." From spending time with her personally and watching her content, I believe it is more than just a willingness to be herself. Dora enjoys being on the platform; she creates serious heartfelt videos but is also seen singing and dancing. She is unwilling to mold herself into what the head of an NGO "should be." "My followers are predominantly women," Dora told me when we discussed the demographic of her followers. She was almost allergic to the word "inspiration" when I probed as to why so many young girls looked up to her. It was clear, though, that she was paving a new way.

"I hate—and I don't use hate a ton—but I hate when people copy other people because we're all so different and so amazingly unique. There's no reason to copy anybody else." She not only had her own unique style and passion for sharing her life and mission, but she also lacked any contemporaries. "I didn't have anyone online or any organization to look at as a blueprint. All of this was new to me and everyone else." Instead of hindering her progress, this allowed her creativity to drive Footprints of Hope. Some of Dora's most popular videos stemmed from last-second ideas right before she filmed. "A lot of times the videos I put the least effort into did the best." She laughed. "It's sort of random but I think those videos connect with people." It wasn't randomness but the nature of human connection. Dora shared spur of the moment happenings at the school and in her life. "Positivity is key because there's so much hurt and so many bad things that happen in the world.

I'm not saying we brush it off, but life shouldn't be as heavy as all that. Sometimes I show the struggles the students go through, but it's also in a positive light. They've been through this, but they're amazing. They're safe here. They're fed and everything is headed in the right direction." Unknowingly, Dora was creating a community of people that were not only interested in funding her endeavors but also quickly becoming a virtual support network.

Her ability to connect deeply with a wide audience translated into fundraising success. Dora's first fundraising campaign raised US$58,618 in only two months. Dora was very specific when recounting this first fundraiser. She didn't say we raised $58k, or almost $60k, she said $58,618—every single dollar mattered. Dora doesn't think in $1 increments, but rather does the mental conversion of each and every dollar to books, eggs for breakfast, or pencils for the classroom. "I remember I was in my house. I was looking for something. And by then my iPhone six was acting up. It was ancient at that point. I went outside and caught a bit of (cell) service. I went to TikTok and I was scrolling and thought, Oh, let me check the GoFundMe. A day or two before we had like seven thousand or seven thousand two hundred. And then the next day, it had gone to fifty-eight thousand, six hundred and eighteen! I remember screaming at first and then feeling very humbled. Just… it was hard for me to comprehend that people would be that generous toward a random person in a remote village." Dora and I were sitting together on her porch. As she told this story it was easy for me to picture her bursting out of her poorly constructed home in elation. Earlier that year she had felt lost and as though her opportunity to create real change had already passed her by. In that moment Dora began to fully comprehend the power she had inside her that had finally connected with the right people.

Her initial impetus for the GoFundMe was to drill boreholes to provide fresh clean water for the school and the surrounding community. "I didn't have any (social) credit… I could have scammed these people and for them to have faith in me and say, 'Here, you do it.' It really meant a lot… I could see the doubt. I am a very intuitive person and both online and throughout my life people have doubted me… so many people." Evelyn, the oldest of Dora's daughters who attended the school, peeked around the corner and interjected. "Mommy, can I go play at the school?" Dora nodded and Evelyn spun around, running in the direction of the school, kicking up dust as she dashed away. Dora's pained smile returned to her face. "I try to ignore the doubt, but it still comes back… And just having these people say, 'Here you go, let's see you do this!'… It meant more than they know."

With over ten times her initial fundraising goal, Dora reached back out to her virtual TikTok community. In a video posted in July of 2020 she updates her followers and asks if her newly established NGO should drill additional boreholes for the greater Mapapa community. Again, she did not have to follow any traditional NGO model; she simply went online to ask for opinions. She went on to explain that any funds left over after the boreholes would be used to build a classroom for the students. From the initial onset of the GoFundMe, Dora was hyper aware of the intense scrutiny she was under. She worked tirelessly to stay transparent about the money coming into Footprints of Hope and exactly where it was being spent. "Every dollar that we receive through the GoFundMe goes to the students. I don't get paid any salary, and the money I live on is from a few individual donors who help me with food and basic necessities for my family." Dora's deep emotional commitment to her mission had been clearly demonstrated to me at so many stages of her journey. If moving into a mud hut with her two adopted daughters to start a school without any funding was not enough, she had carried this spirit forward by not accepting a salary.

Setting out to drill five boreholes in a community that lacked access to potable drinking water was a new endeavor for Dora. She had experience working in large mission organizations, but she had never been the sole person responsible with a project of this size. "It was really frustrating, because we had a limited choice of who to work with... and then the company we did choose to put in the boreholes ended up charging us when they made a mistake on where to drill. I really thought that getting the boreholes drilled and pumps installed would be this big moment where I felt a wave of success, but by the end I was actually really frustrated and just relieved to have them in." I was surprised to hear that this wasn't a triumphant moment for her and her newly established NGO. The more we spoke about this time, the more Dora opened up about the external pressure she was under. "You know all these people donated money to have something done and even though the company made a mistake and the project was going to cost more, I couldn't come back to these people with excuses. They paid to see this happen and I felt like I absolutely needed to get that done." The pressure to produce trickled down from all levels of the online world. She wanted not only to prove the doubters wrong but also felt an enormous responsibility to those who had faith in her.

Instead of sharing these frustrations and concerns with her audience, Dora battled privately. She focused on the positive, sharing the strides she and the children had begun to make. Shortly after installing the final boreholes, Dora caught wind that the villagers were not using them. "I found out that people in the village were saying I cursed, or that I had poisoned the boreholes... I had put in so much work and energy into getting them installed and now people were spreading these rumors." It was a common thread during those early days; each step forward Dora made with her online community often would create more doubt from her surrounding community. While I sympathized greatly with Dora, I could see how the rural community of Mapapa would have cause for doubt. This woman living in abject poverty somehow had the money to feed and educate the village's children. Now Dora had gone a step further and installed wells for everyone. If you didn't have any insight into Dora's background or funding source, the whole operation did seem, well, like magic.

Dora, to her immense credit, handled this rumor like we should all handle rumors. She simply and directly addressed the issues at hand and refused to engage with any subsequent and hateful chatter. She spoke at a village meeting during the weeks following the installation of the boreholes. "I was very frustrated. I had a lot going on and the last thing I had time for was coaxing these people to use something I had worked so hard to get for them. I basically told them 'It's there, go ahead and use it. If you don't or you think I'm a witch, you're *Ubufotini*, which means ignorant." The villagers that appreciated what she was trying to accomplish also voiced their opposition to the hurtful rumors. Dora was not impervious to her community's pushback. Instead of receiving immense gratitude, she was on the defensive as she fought to establish rapport with her neighbors.

It was a Wednesday morning in October. Classes had just begun and the students could be heard reciting the alphabet and calling out answers to the various teachers. Rounding the corner of the library, I nearly collided with Evans. He had grown significantly since I first met him and was nearing eye level to me. Despite his newfound height, his face and lanky body reminded me of his real age: fifteen. Evans was one of the boys I spent the most time with because he had been at the school for a while. Despite being at the school for two years, he still had difficulty understanding most of my daily questions, but when he did understand his face would light up and he would begin to share a drawn-out answer. As I stepped back to avoid bumping into him, we both laughed. "Teacher Dora is requesting you in the dining hall," he reported through a wide smile. The two of us wove through the small trees growing around the classroom block to arrive at the dining hall. Evans left as I entered the door and I sat across from Dora, notebook in hand.

"What's on the program for today?" Dora asked as I opened my notebook. It was her way of giving me an opening for a few morning questions before she would unload everything that needed to be accomplished that day. This morning I was less bold than usual and instead of launching into my usual deluge, I sat back and told her how great a kid Evans was. After having spent many weeks together, Dora knew I was likely asking to hear a bit more about him. It wasn't just his past that I was interested in but also his growth and adjustment at the school. He was in fact one of her earliest students. Evans, along with Dora, had gone through this two-year journey, and his future was largely dependent on the success of Dora's mission.

Evans was born into a family of twelve children, eight girls and four boys. His parents, the same mother and father of all twelve children, lived just a few kilometers away from Footprints of Hope. His early life reflects that of many of the children now attending the school. Both of his parents worked on a large farm earning no more than 70 kwacha a day or the equivalent of US$2. "His parents weren't abusive. They just didn't take care of him. Evans was neglected." As we sat together Dora reflected on the life of a young boy I had grown to appreciate. His life story wasn't a dramatic one; rather, it was unfortunately typical of many of the boys at the school. "When I met Evans, he was wandering around the village looking for food. He would go fishing at the dam and if he didn't catch anything he wouldn't eat that day." When the school first opened Evans was one of the first kids in line for the free meals. "At first we had a lot of trouble with him... Evans had trouble with authority and was always fighting to be first in line for food. He was also very emotionally closed off." As Dora continued talking about this initial period, it was hard to imagine this behavior from the boy I knew. Evans was a model student. He was kind and was always seen taking the younger kids under his wing. After leaving on my first visit he wrote me a letter, signing off with "I hope to see you soon Teacher Joe, Love Evans."

Dora wasn't just dealing with one difficult case during the initial period of opening the school. "Every one of our students comes from a situation that puts them at a big disadvantage." It was something everyone online also knew. Each of these children had their own battle and despite being in a safe place, their future wasn't necessarily secured either. Being physically at the school helped me begin to understand Footprints of Hope not through an organizational lens but as individual stories bound to one person: Teacher Dora.

Chapter 12

Shifting the Prado into park, I turned to Dora. "Indian food?" she said. I laughed. Perhaps she was beginning to know me too well. We were in Kabwe, a city three hours south of the school, running errands and picking up donation packages. Zambia, despite being in landlocked Africa, has a large population of Indian and Pakistani people. This ethnic group stems from the initial traders that came here from their homeland at the turn of the twentieth century seeking economic opportunity. Unlike in East and South Africa, these initial migrants were skilled artisans and businesspeople.[15] Most migrants to other parts of Africa from the same region of the

---

[15] From Kings Cross to Kew: Following the History of Zambia's Indian Community through British Imperial Archives, *History in Africa*, Haig, Joan M. 2007

world were predominantly indentured laborers. Despite their small population, this ethnic group plays a large role in trade, transportation, and hospitality. During my time in Zambia, I enjoyed some of the most delicious Indian and Pakistani food I've had in my life. It was a common bond between Dora and me, our love for this delicious comfort food. I followed her into the restaurant where we ordered some takeaway and Dora exchanged small talk with the owner, a longtime friend.

Spending time in Kabwe with Dora felt a bit like returning to a friend's old high school. Having heard many of her young adult stories, I could now imagine them unfolding in the physical location. Her adoption of Veronica and Mary, the isolation she felt working for bosses who overlooked her, and a feeling that her life's mission was passing her by. Walking toward the large grocery store, Dora and I were stopped by a group of young girls in black high school uniforms. "Are you Dora from TikTok?" they asked excitedly. The girls huddled together with Dora and I snapped a photo. Unbeknownst to them, Dora had attended the same high school they did. Dora always made time for these people, especially young women. It was part of her larger outreach, even though she only saw it as "I'm just being kind, it's the human thing to do. We should encourage those girls."

As Dora continued to share her life online, her presence

began to mushroom. This online image of Dora and Footprints of Hope was filled with a positive outlook despite the difficulties in Mapapa. On the ground, however, progress at the school continued to be slow despite the growing movement to fund her organization. Dora had never been solely responsible for a project of this magnitude. Having just turned twenty-eight, this was not surprising, yet those who knew Dora recognized her dedication and passion to ensure the school succeeded. "Dora is very stubborn when she has an idea and it involves helping someone that has less. She won't quit easily," her friend Simunza told me when we spoke over the phone. It was late in the afternoon after Dora and I had returned to Mapapa. I was hunched over a picnic table sweating as I spoke to this longtime friend of Dora's. It was clear that her friends and family were not surprised by her growing success during this time. While speaking with her community and family, I could never shake the fact that Dora to a large extent didn't really feel their support. Many like Simunza and Dora's childhood friends were busy with lives of their own, but it was also more than that. "A lot of people in Zambia get mad when they see someone else succeed. A lot of people pull each other down here. There are even songs that we dance to that talk about when one black person sees another succeed, it's because they went to a witch doctor…. It's tough because people are positive when you are struggling, but then get mad at your success," Dora told me when I questioned the doublespeak I heard from various groups. It wasn't only Dora who relayed this sentiment; the other teachers had explained song lyrics and shared anecdotes of similar stories. Jealousy seems to only be quelled if the party in question can monetize the friendship, despite not supporting Dora during her most difficult periods. I knew that this type of behavior isolated Dora socially and made her wary of so-called "friends."

Reflecting on her preparedness, Dora felt she had spent three years learning, training, and waiting for this opportunity while working for other organizations. She knew the dangers that came with overextending her resources and overpromising to both her donors and the community. Within the first six months of creating her TikTok account, Dora had amassed a following of over 600,000 followers. It was no small feat, and even more important was the faith and encouragement that the online community fueled her with. "Early on it was difficult when we would face setbacks and delays at the school because everyone that had given money… well, they don't really care about excuses and delays. These people donated all this money and they wanted to see it being used to accomplish our goal." Even as I spoke to Dora almost two years later, those feelings remained. There was always a sense of urgency at the school. Progress—more specifically, physical progress that could be shared via TikTok—was vital to maintain donations. This weighed heavily on Dora. It meant that there was always something to be working on and sharing via social media. The constant stream of updates could not be paused, even for a day.

After her first seven months of posting and working publicly on establishing Footprints of Hope, Dora made a breakthrough. "I was outside cooking and I got a notification on my phone. It was from the official TikTok page and when I opened my account I saw a blue checkmark." Dora's account had officially been "verified" by the social media platform. "I was so excited, I grabbed Grace and started jumping up and down and shouting." A video Dora shared just moments after she received the news documents an exultant Dora jumping around and excitedly updating her followers. Standing side by side with her daughter Mary, it was a full circle moment. Seven months prior the two had made their initial video together and now it had grown into a movement.

Verification on a social media platform means simply that the platform, in this case TikTok, states that the identity of the user has been confirmed. It "verifies" the user as an "online celebrity" or "public figure."[16] This badge of honor is not tied to

---

[16] How to tell if an account is verified, Tiktok Newsroom Aug. 29 2019

a certain follower count but is based on the amount of public attention a person attracts. This attention is calculated based on search engine data and news articles distributed about the public figure. Despite no official records, Dora was the first Zambian we could find who had been verified on TikTok. I would often tease Dora, calling her an influencer or online celebrity. She balked at the notion. "Yea, I think I will partner with a makeup brand next and start doing lifestyle vlogs," she said, miming with a peace sign and extending her phone outward in a pretend selfie. It was all somewhat tongue in cheek humor between the two of us, knowing full well that this platform was in fact her livelihood. At the time of verification, Dora had officially become the "village TikToker" as she referred to herself. Her online village of TikTok followers enabled her to drive physical changes in the village of Mapapa and the lives of its children.

Dora also worked to build her first classroom. This initial classroom was crude and admittedly below even the more remote village standards for Zambian schools. Using burnt mud bricks that she fired from her own oven, they built a classroom that was half thatch and half walls of burnt bricks. Although it was far from the standard Dora strived for, it was nonetheless a respite from the relentless sun and a place for her students to call their school. During the rains the classroom would flood and students' artwork that adorned the walls often needed replacing. Videos of this on her page share the realities of this time, but also the happiness of her students who for the first time began learning from a passionate, qualified educator. "The first classroom was structurally not sound, but it took us from nothing to a school and I'm grateful for that." When it came to building, Dora had a lot to learn, and these initial projects were destined to be placeholders until greater funding could be acquired.

A cool breeze passed through the open window and the paper chains hanging from the A-frame rafters began to rustle. Teacher Thandiwe, six months pregnant, sat in front of a group of children. The second-grade class sat cross-legged, squeezed onto a foam mat in the corner of the classroom. Each student eyed their instructor in anticipation of the next flashcard she would present. Thandiwe projected toward the class, "A is for?" "Aaaaa," the students shouted back in unison. She smiled and praised them before moving on to the next flashcard. Sitting on a low wooden couch, I watched the lesson unfold. The students shot me furtive glances throughout as I nodded approvingly while they worked through the English lesson. Many of these students had only been learning English for a few months. Thandiwe herself joined the school in October of 2020 when her curiosity about Dora forced her to walk through the yellow gates for the first time.

"I was working at SeedCo at the time and I heard about this woman who was clothing, feeding, and educating these village children. I was told she was a satanist and I thought to myself, I should go and meet that satanist." She burst out laughing. Thandiwe loved to laugh, and it was this energy that initially connected with Dora. During my extended stays at Footprints of Hope I spent many hours with Thandiwe. She was constantly found by Dora's side, often writing lists of supplies and rattling off tasks that still needed attention. Thandiwe, like all the staff at Footprints of Hope, was young, only twenty-eight. She was born just a few kilometers east of the school to a single mother of a large family; Thandiwe's mother was a subsistence farmer. Thandiwe grew up in a modest village home with no running water or electricity. It was school and a desire to learn that became her greatest opportunity. Thandiwe's mother put a focus on her daughter's education, knowing it would be her best chance at a more economically prosperous life.

Age twenty-six, Thandiwe was working at SeedCo, the large farm bloc that dominates the landscape for miles. Day in and day out she worked to count bags of maize and record figures for the farm's record books. It was menial work and did little to insight passion. "I wanted a different job, and I heard about Teacher Dora from a friend on my way home from work. I passed that friend my resume to give to Dora." This resume fell on deaf ears at Footprints of Hope. Dora then and now is impressed by action. Again, Thandiwe sent word to Dora asking if she was interested. No response. Finally, she showed up at the gates of Footprints of Hope and requested a meeting with Dora. "I was really busy that day and needed to go to Kabwe to pick up some donations because at the time things were getting stolen a lot," Dora told me. Thandiwe, now in real pursuit of the opportunity, told Dora she was also going to Kabwe and that she would join her. The two set off and during their journey they began to get acquainted. "When I met Teacher Dora I was like, oh my English is not good enough," she said with a laugh. Dora was unlike the people Thandiwe was surrounded by. She was a single adoptive mother, better educated, and more traveled. Instead of being unnerved, Thandiwe focused on being herself and enjoyed their conversation the best she could.

"It was an interesting day. I sort of thought she was a little crazy," Dora recalled.

The next morning Grace came running up to Dora. "The new teacher is starting her lesson with the children."

Confused, Dora turned to her daughter. "What new teacher?"

Walking from her home across the yard to the thatched classroom, Dora realized that instead of waiting to be offered the position, Thandiwe had just taken it for herself. "It was as if she just started on her own. I needed the help and she was willing to learn, so it became a natural fit." The school staff now grew to four employees—three female teachers and a male security guard for the evenings. For the girls and women of the village it was a new sight to behold. A group of young women building, educating, and feeding a group of children as well as instructing the men as to how they should complete tasks on the property. When I asked about this, it always put wide, devilish grins on their faces, proud of being the "bwana" of their own domain.

The relationship between Thandiwe and Dora quickly developed into a friendship. I admired Thandiwe's ability to be both Dora's friend while also recognizing the great deal she could learn from Dora. This dynamic plays out regularly at the isolated school. Teachers are far removed from the nearest city and have to look to one another for socialization and friendship outside of class. Working at Footprints of Hope is no doubt demanding. The teachers seem to be constantly working even when not in class. As funding allowed for new teachers to be hired, the student body began to grow. Dora worked intimately with women in the village to identify at-risk children, specifically girls, and bring them to the school. Women in the village who came from abusive homes or had little economic opportunity were hired and trained as aunties and caretakers. The first year of the school, the entire staff except the security guard was made up of women. It was a cornerstone of the example Dora strived to set. Zambian women could create their own destiny and escape even the direst situations. It wasn't until one of the men helping burn bricks was properly introduced to Dora that Footprints of Hope would welcome its first male teacher, Teacher Victor.

Teacher Victor walked two paces ahead of me, his long strides extending through the bush as we walked through the village in the midmorning heat. Earlier, I had spoken to him and expressed my interest in walking over to the hospital Dora was currently fundraising to build. Over the course of my time at Footprints of Hope, Victor and I had become friends. He turned to me. "You remember us driving through here to harvest the soybeans?" He nodded, gesturing to the narrow dirt road. "Yes, I was worried about my radiator blowing up that whole afternoon!" I laughed. I enjoyed spending time with Victor outside of the school; it was an opportunity for me to see a different part of him. Seeing him interact with members of the community was a reminder that he was, despite his clothes and stoic nature, one of them himself.

Victor was born in Kamanda, the village just a few meters beyond the gates of Footprints of Hope. His parents are in their seventies, faces wrinkled from years working as subsistence farmers in the field to support their nine children. Unlike Thandiwe, Victor's family home and community slowly revealed themselves during each subsequent visit to the school. My respect for him only grew during our conversations while driving to neighboring villagers' homes on errands or picking up goods in Masansa. I also met his sister Prudence, who worked at the school.

"Joe, do you think you will move to Zambia permanently?" Victor asked, pitching his head to the side. It was a question that caught me solidly off guard.

"I'm not sure. I think I have more to see before I think about moving anywhere permanently, to be honest," I replied.

His lips pressed together, he gave me a single head nod. "You know what Teacher Dora has accomplished here. It is very impressive. Before she came and installed the boreholes the situation was very bad. It had been a dry season and I don't think the surface wells would have enough water for the crops. Many people would be in a bad situation." As he spoke I nodded, eagerly accepting information I knew Dora was too humble to speak about openly. "She is very impressive. She has done so much for the community. I am proud to work at the school and be a part of it." Saying this, it was as though he was talking to the footpath rather than me, directing his voice onward, deeper into the village.

"My father worked for a white farmer when I was very young. The white farmer always told my dad that his children needed to focus on learning at school. My father respected him and after he lost his job, he still made it a point to have us learn." Victor's family moved from another part of the Luano district, some thirty to forty kilometers, to Kamanda after his father lost his job. From this point forward, his family would subsist on what they could grow. Victor's oldest brother, Golden, was his role model. After graduating secondary school, Golden struck out on his own and was able to work and grind his way through college. During this time, he reached out to Victor and had him move into a small apartment in Kabwe. The two shared a few difficult years together. Working, studying, and scraping by, Golden graduated college and landed an excellent government job in Lusaka. Victor's nature made it hard to tell if the two were close emotionally, but I imagined they had to be. Golden had guided and helped fund Victor's education. Victor himself never intended to be a teacher, but other options were not in budget so for the time being he threw himself into learning to be a secondary school math teacher. "I wanted to be an accountant too, but at the time we couldn't afford the classes. Going to teaching college made sense and I knew I could get a good job." As he said this, he seemed content with his decision based on the school and community he had once again landed in.

The more time we spent together the easier it was to get to know this reserved man who was just two years my senior. As a twenty-seven-year-old unmarried college educated man, he was no doubt in the minority in the village. I would often prod him about this in a joking manner which he would receive with a trademark heavy breath through the nose and a wide grin. The more I learned about Victor, the more his relationship with the community around him became clear. Footprints of Hope, and even teaching for that matter, weren't inherently important to him. It was the work and leadership Dora entrusted within him that was his driving concern. It was not hard to imagine Victor being one of the students at the school himself. The first time he met Dora he was sweating over an oven, burning dozens of bricks while at home from school. "I made bricks to help supplement my school fees and help my family. That's how I met Teacher Dora." The two slowly became acquainted as he sold her extra blocks for the new buildings.

"I hired Victor because of his character," Dora told me about her decision to bring him on. "I saw him working and funding his education. He was different and showed a lot of respect to me, which is rare among men in the village."

Over the course of the following year, Teacher Victor would grow into his role not only as the school's math teacher but also as a role model. Sitting in his classroom during the hot afternoons, I saw that the children, particularly the older boys, watched his every move. His approval and acknowledgment of their efforts painted broad smiles across their faces that seemed to last for minutes. Teacher Victor represented the man these young boys could hopefully someday emulate. He made mistakes but was willing to acknowledge them and work forward. His deep respect for Dora and ability to work underneath Thandiwe displayed his views of equality among the genders. "He is really respectful, and it's something that isn't generally taught in the village. He's a great example for the children, especially the boys who are always watching. They know that he's from the same place as them and that they can be like him too," Dora told me.

Returning to the school after a three-week absence, I learned that Victor had finally moved into the staff housing. It was welcome news. Teacher Victor was already a pillar at Footprints of Hope but was now a constant figure beyond just in the classroom. I told him this and he responded with a wide smile and a head nod, not saying a single word. When I met Victor, he had been living in his parents' very modest home. They had no running water and had a small solar unit that could power a few light bulbs and charge a phone. I'll never forget being completely baffled as to how he came to work each morning with a pressed shirt despite living in a mud and thatch house. Teacher Victor, in some ways, will always be an enigma to me. His drive and honesty were why he wanted to work at the school. Dora was more than an organization, a social media presence, or a fundraiser; to many, she was an opportunity. To Victor, and others, she offered a chance to be the change they so desperately needed.

Chapter 13

At the end of a long day filled with errands, meetings, and tasks of all sorts Dora knocked on my door. I was staying in the modest guest house/storage room across the yard from her own home. I stepped out onto the porch and joined her on the plastic chairs in front. Time ran differently at Footprints of Hope. One of Dora's daughters or a student would often bound up to me and report a change in schedule. "Teacher Dora says make it five o'clock," or "Teacher Dora says to meet her at the gate now." Often disconnected from the internet and only able to write, it wasn't unusual for me to be scrambling to meet Dora or staring at a blank page for another forty-five minutes due to a delay. This evening I had not expected her to be able to meet but was pleasantly surprised by the chance to continue a conversation that had been cut short. "So you want to know how the community feels about me now?" she said, raising her eyebrows with a devilish grin.

The community Dora worked to serve maintained a rocky relationship with both her and the organization. From the moment she first began laying the foundation of her mud hut and teaching the village children, pushback from the community started. Despite this, there were early supporters. "There were some village women and a few men that even early on did try and say nice things and lend support," she said as I swatted mosquitoes away from my face. The population of Mapapa is almost entirely subsistence farmers. Few people have beyond a 6th grade education, and most have never traveled further than the village boundaries.[17] Men dominate within the home and in civil society. A single adoptive mother occupying this domain with her own agenda didn't sit well with many. "It was so difficult at first because it felt like just about everyone was against me... The GoFundMe really helped me push forward, but it was still hard. People online didn't have any idea of how hard it was here in Mapapa for me." She never admitted to wavering, but it was clear that her confidence and self-esteem were brutally low during the early days.

---

[17] Education in Zambia, UNICEF Zambia Country Program 2021

Things began to take a turn as Dora brought on more teachers. Thandiwe, Mawinee, and Victor added local voices to her work. They acted as an unofficial PR team, dispelling myths and working to share the mission the school promoted. I asked about Dora's emotions as the cultural tide began to turn in her favor ever so slightly. It was nearly impossible for me to comprehend the unique pressure witchcraft and satanic accusations had on the young woman seated across from me. Speaking about it now, she would almost roll her eyes about the rumors, but it was also still clear that they had hurt her.

Getting up to leave, Dora turned and said, "Eight am tomorrow we'll leave to meet the chief. Do you have the chief's interview questions ready?"

Before heading to bed that evening, I sat underneath the blinding solar light. It was so hard to articulate the pain, exhaustion, and joy Dora shared only through her facial expressions. Her setbacks and small victories in Mapapa over the past year could not be summarized in a few words. It's not our vocabulary or language skills that hold these conversations back but an inability to properly share an experience that likely must be lived rather than read. Like days at the school when the sun's heat rose steadily, cultural change in Mapapa was hard to notice, the same way the heat was bearable until sweat dripping off my chin splattered across my notepad.

Dora couldn't quantify the change that had slowly occurred in Mapapa; she was too close and too focused on the future.

"Wow, you look very handsome, Teacher Joe!" Teacher Thandiwe said as I joined her on Dora's porch the next morning.

"Thank you, Teacher Thandiwe. You look very beautiful this morning!" We both laughed. Greetings like this are so customary at the school, but the nature of them is never lost on us. I was wearing the nicest outfit I had brought to Zambia: a white button-down safari-type shirt and black hiking pants. It was a far cry from the suit and Allen Edmond leather monk shoes that would have qualified as formalwear at my last job. Teacher Dora joined us outside. The two women immediately made me feel underdressed, as usual.

"Who's ready to meet with the chief?" Dora asked as we piled into the car. The chief's official palace was a long drive from Footprints of Hope, but one I was now familiar with, having met him a few months earlier. During our first visit, I was surprised by the simplicity of His Royal Highness Chief Chikupili's palace and his appearance. Chief Chikupili oversees the Luano district and rules over the Swaka people. During that first meeting, Dora, Thandiwe, Gant Chibuye (the chief's secretary), and I were all kneeling in a straw hut as the chief emerged. We greeted him in a traditional manner by cupping our hands and clapping off to the side of our bodies when he walked into the room. The chief had a casual manner and sported a large black winter coat and black baseball hat. "I'm pleased to meet you, Joseph," he said as I introduced myself. Dora explained why I had joined them and asked for an audience in a few months for me to interview him. He readily agreed, noting, "The work Dora is doing with those children is very important."

During our initial meeting, I found Chief Chikupili to be quite amiable. I couldn't, however, wrap my head around why the locals spoke highly of him at the school. They were essentially forced to give him gifts of money and a vehicle just so that they could feed, clothe, house, and educate the vulnerable members of his kingdom. I thought their approval of him was more of a contrived calculation than a natural response to a system that was clearly exploiting them. When I pointed this out to Dora she acquiesced, backtracking on some of her earlier statements. "Yes, it is really frustrating that we are doing the work he should be doing or at least helping with, but the reality is that it could be so much worse. In other places in Zambia many of the chiefs would constantly be at our gate asking for gifts or money. He is supportive of our mission and accepts the generous gifts we give but doesn't ask for more." Although Chief Chikupili may have been more progressive than some of the other chiefs throughout Zambia, it remained a hard pill to swallow, knowing donation money and gifts were presented to nothing more than a figurehead.

Dora works within the system to accomplish her goals at the school and in the community. It means that there were some things she doesn't share with donors. "It's hard because we do have to spend money on things like gifts and expenses that are largely unseen, but it's also the only way to push our mission forward. I don't think that people who donate would understand if I made a thirty-second video trying to explain all of this." I agreed that many of the "expenses" of doing business in Zambia were nothing more than an inducement for someone to do the job they were already paid to do. I held my tongue more than once as Dora paid additional fees or paid employees a tip for doing what was objectively their obligation in their current role. To the world, Dora is doing the lifesaving work of a humanitarian, educator, and single mother. As I trailed behind her during our months together, I watched a woman operate in an environment and within a system that a foreigner would be lost in. Dora is able to navigate through the complex political, commercial, and cultural system in a way that showcases, despite her protestations, that she truly is a Zambian leader.

Meeting the chief for the second time, I was eager to ask

him about his educational background and his impression of Dora and Footprints of Hope. I did, however, know that I was to tread lightly. At the end of the day, he had direct control over the land rights and happenings within his kingdom. I needed to be cognizant of and maintain Dora's positive relationship with him. Dora was traveling with legal documents to request that Chief Chikupili "liberate" the land that Footprints of Hope stands on. As mentioned earlier, Zambia is divided into kingdoms, each of which is overseen by a chief. Within the chiefdom all the land is legally owned by the chief. Residents of the kingdom can rent or buy the land they live and farm on. Even though they "own" this land it still legally belongs to the chief should he wish to reclaim it for any purpose. The caveat to this system is land that is legally "liberated" and relinquished by the chief and unless sold back to him is outside his purview. To an outsider it's hard to understand buying a piece of land twice, first from the family in the village that "owns" it and then again from the chief. Most villagers never have a need to liberate their land and even should they want to, would not have the money or wherewithal to get through the process. It seemed like a system of contrived private ownership that was reserved for people with money—basically anyone but the villagers. According to many I spoke with, the system works well in the village. The chief acts as a judge of sorts, settling disputes and working to ensure those in his village, even the poorest, have enough land to farm food to subsist on. I made a genuine effort to remain open to this system of governance that was antithetical to the Western approach of private property. It was critical to remind myself that for the people in Luano District, this system is as ancient as the ground they stand on.

The car bounded forward as the two teachers and I surfed the thick sand toward the chief's official residence. "Thandiwe, do you have the gift for the chief?" Dora said, turning to the back seat. Thandiwe smiled and pulled out a wad of cash. "Let's make an envelope or something for it," Dora said as she ripped a page out of my notepad, folding it into a makeshift wrapper. We arrived at the palace just as the chief was planning to leave. Unfortunately, another Zambian chief had passed away and it was Chikupili's duty to visit the family and mourn with them. Upon seeing us, his guard, dressed in plain clothes and whose name was also Joseph, pulled up a few plastic chairs. Joseph stepped behind the chief's chair and our meeting began.

This second encounter was far more casual and again the chief was warm and welcoming to me. "I became chief in 2013. My job here is to stay with the people and work on development. They are my subjects and I settle disputes and work with the headmen to oversee the people." He spoke slowly in a soft tone as he looked directly at me. He explained that the kingdom has a population of about five thousand residents and he oversees eighty-two headmen. These headmen, some of whom I had met in passing, worked with specific villages and were the extended arm of the chief himself. "Yeah... in terms of challenges we face Hospitals is a big one. We don't have a hospital yet. We are just using Masansa," he said, referring to the small hospital I had visited many times with Dora.

Our conversation continued in a somewhat staccato manner as I phrased and rephrased questions that were misunderstood. The chief seemed to circle around many things I asked. It was apparent that he wasn't avoiding questions but was confused by some of the words, such as "vision" and "timeline." Rephrasing and even at points letting Thandiwe translate into Bemba, we continued. "For me, I want the girls to avoid early marriages.... We don't want these young girls to marry. I want these girls to go to school.... Even you have come to write and help. I say to Madam Dora, build even more places to help our kingdom. What do you think, Madam?" He smiled and Dora leaned forward and said, "If you give us money, we will come!" We all let out a laugh.

The chief was patient and extremely respectful to me, a foreigner with no official status and just a long list of questions. Chief Chikupili had no obligation to me or to help me understand his role. Halfway through the interview, he turned to Dora and nodded toward her and said, "I was told about Madam here by the headman and then after that she came to visit me so that we could meet and talk about her project." He was referring to the period in which Dora was first starting the school and had received money for the boreholes. Chief Chikupli had the same respect for Dora that I did. He likely couldn't have cared less about the interview or whatever my goal was that day. He was entertaining me solely as a favor to a person he seemed to genuinely respect. To me, his body language and manners toward Dora were as important as anything he could have told me during our interview.

Almost a year and a half earlier, Dora had come, hat in hand, to a man whom she had a greater education than, more development experience, and objectively a more global perspective. She, however, was not born into a royal family. Rather than focusing on the fact that she was doing this man and his kingdom a favor, Dora remained humble. It's a trait few leaders truly possess. You know more, you can achieve more, and yet you need the approval of someone who, albeit less educated, still is a potential roadblock. The way in which Dora interacts with the chief, headman, and government officials in Zambia is a display of her commitment to the children she serves, not Zambia or its system of government. Dora looks at the chief, the Luano District, and the country with far different eyes than a foreigner ever could. Instead of becoming jaded by a system which doesn't serve her, she understands that the knowledge of this bureaucracy is an asset in itself. Once, during a conversation about her time working for a mission organization, Dora told me, "I had experience. It just wasn't what they were looking for." Dora was the odd one out, a black Zambian woman who had more to offer in terms of practical experience than the rest of the room combined. Despite her deficit in education compared to her foreign counterparts, Dora has something they would never be able to obtain. She has cultural, political, and social ties to this place she has called home her entire life.

As we ended our meeting with the chief, he stood. The three of us moved to kneel and before we could, he waved us off. He approached me and I bent at the waist in a slight bow as I clasped his hand. He thanked me again for the work I was doing and bid the ladies farewell. I climbed into the driver's seat and Dora reviewed the paperwork she had received from the chief to liberate the land. It was a monumental day. Footprints of Hope was going to be more independent than ever. I asked Dora how she felt about what she had just accomplished. Ignoring my opening for some self-congratulation, she said, "I think we all need to focus on helping wherever we can, with whatever skills we have. People just need to be kind to one another."

When Dora said this, I suddenly felt small. The school, the teachers, and even Dora are all far from perfect, but they strive to be better. It is a common bond that links all the workers at the school. In some way or another, everyone has something to prove. Throughout her entire life, Dora has tried to achieve things that people explicitly said were unobtainable for her. Whenever she speaks about the proverbial "bigger picture" it is in an almost utopian fashion. She isn't naive about the world, far from it. Dora knows more intimately than most people the evil things humans do to one another. But she has a steadfast unwillingness to compromise her belief that every child has a right to being fed, clothed, educated, and loved. If that is a utopian vision for this world, then everyone else is crazy, not her.

Spirits were high on the drive home. In Masansa we made two short stops, and I secured us some fritters. Thandiwe and I now had a tradition of always stopping to eat a few together when in Masansa. These six-cent donuts were a local favorite of ours. Dora would roll her eyes, always telling us the people who cook them never wash their hands or the dishes. "That's what makes them so tasty!" I replied, to which Thandiwe let out a cackle as she finished eating her second. Back on the road, it was a straight-shot forty-five minutes back to the school. Rolling down the windows, Dora blasted Backstreet Boys and

Black-Eyed Peas and we all sang along. The car bobbed up and down, and without our seatbelts we would have been airborne. As I sang along and watched the joy on Dora and Thandiwe's faces, the immensity of what they were accomplishing once again washed over me.

Chapter 14

"Are you at the red gate?" Dora asked over the phone. "Ummm, I don't really know… all three are sort of… oh wait I see you!" Dora waved with a warm open smile. She escorted the car through the gate as I drove up to a small house within the compound. A shiny blue wheelchair, which was more of a mobility seat that needed a second person to push it, sat outside the building. It was my first time seeing Dora in Lusaka, a city where she spent much of her early years. We were far from Mutendere where she grew up, but the area, despite being safe, wasn't exactly Kabulonga. Kabulonga is a neighborhood within the city dominated by expats and wealthy Zambians. As a young woman running a large NGO, Dora could have justified staying just about anywhere in the city.

But she chose a place that had the rates permanently engraved into the hotel sign: 200 kwacha (US$12.50) a night. Unlocking and lifting the fiberglass cover on the bed of my truck, I began lifting her suitcases and the wheelchair in. "Who is the wheelchair for?" I asked. "It's for a young boy in the village who currently doesn't have one. He doesn't attend our school, but you know." She smiled with her trademark grin. We both laughed. Dora's generosity is impossible for her to contain. From an organizational perspective, she is working on being more disciplined and having a framework for what kinds of intervention she can spend on. Sort of ironic, I thought. Most people worry about cutting spending on personal items whereas Dora is trying to stop impulse-buying life-changing supplies for kids. Thandiwe and Dora's lawyer was reminding her to be more frugal about these random acts of kindness.

Dora has deep gratitude for her life and the resources now at her disposal. Just a year and a half earlier, in December of 2020, the walls of her own house had collapsed. The aftermath was, of course, shown online. Despite the shocking nature of the disaster, Dora remained calm. "I don't think people fully realize, but when I moved to the village I was all in. I moved my girls, my life—I was totally committed. A lot of the setbacks were really tough, but there wasn't even an option to quit. How could I leave this place now?" Gratitude was a grounding principle that kept Dora in Mapapa. It was easy for her to look around and see how much she had, largely because just months earlier, she had almost nothing and many of the children only had her. It was this ability to take stock, both in past events and the progress of her students, that enabled this gratitude.

In early 2021, she had a growing online fan base and donations continued to increase, but Dora's focus had remained narrow: building classrooms and housing for the students. Sharing the experience online was a reminder to her one million followers that her journey and personal stability was still a precarious balance. "I just wanted to make sure that we had a place for the children to learn and be safe. Our house was not built right (referring to the building standard) from the beginning because I didn't know enough about building at the time…. After it collapsed, it was time to build something bigger and stronger," Dora told me. Supervising the entire teaching staff, serving as the de facto social worker to 105 students, managing a social media presence, and legitimizing her organization, Dora had an enormous amount of responsibility on her shoulders. The pressure was also mounting: 2021 was a year of immense growth for the school physically and for Dora personally.

Dora worked on building her first "safe house" or "hostel,"

names she used interchangeably before landing on "dormitory." Dora's vision for what she was accomplishing was finally beginning to match language reserved for schools and organizations that far exceeded the small operation she once had. These green buds sprouting from the tree she had planted were markers of the transformation Footprints of Hope was going through as an organization. The impetus for the dormitory was to provide a permanent and safe housing option for children escaping abuse. In a TikTok posted in March of 2021, while the building was under construction, Dora spoke openly about the struggles she was having. "My biggest problem with building here is not the funding," she said, showing viewers the foundation of a half-built dormitory, "it's that there are no reliable people." Dora began to explain the issues with the sixteen men she originally hired for the construction job: "They brought prostitution… consuming substances was a thing and I don't allow that… they undermined me… I'm very stuck at the moment. Everything seems so hard right now." It was a broken video; her words and thoughts seemed to tumble out and then falter. She was sharing a real moment that was felt by viewers around the world. Despite not seeing her face, it was hard not to sympathize with a woman who was likely thousands of miles from most of her viewers.

Driving through Lusaka, we headed to Kamwala market. Our task that afternoon was to pick up six large reams of fabric that would be turned into student uniforms. As we sat in traffic, Dora updated me on the children. I always asked about Nandi first. How was she adjusting? Any updates on her court case? Was her speech impediment improving with Dora's coaching? The pace of things in Zambia is slow, but Dora's work with the children is not. She threw herself into investing in their lives and ensuring that they knew that neither she nor the other teachers were going to leave them. This allowed me to see the transformation of many children. Kids that had initially arrived at Footprints of Hope shy and afraid would gain confidence and become chatterboxes over the weeks and months I visited. Dora was humble about her involvement but rivaled the proudest grandparent imaginable with the length at which she could talk about "her kids." She referred to all her students as her children. "Everyone is doing really well… donations have slowed though... I just... I wish we didn't have to constantly worry about money." It was a part of her job that needed attention and took a huge amount of time. Donations had to be constantly flowing in. Without a steady stream of funds, the school would only last for a few months on savings before being forced to shutter its doors.

Zambia's annual GDP per capita hovers around US$1,050.

Globally, Zambia has some of the highest rates of poverty and inequality in the world, according to the World Bank.[18] It's a misperception held by many who have never set foot in the country that due to the extremely low levels of income, goods and services would be cheap. It's quite the contrary, because Zambia is a landlocked nation. Most goods sold within the country are imported and thus must be shipped across the continent and are subject to high import taxes. For Dora, this problem is exacerbated by the need to ship building supplies to a remote village. Hiring well-trained craftsmen is also difficult as education among the trades and skilled workers remains low. She has to offer transportation or even housing to these workers, who are almost always men. In a normal week together, I would witness Dora pulling out stacks of cash to pay for transport of materials and hundreds to fill her Prado with gas in order to transport children, food, and supplies. "I'm a drug dealer!" she would joke as she pulled out thick stacks of kwacha notes. Ironically, I don't think Dora ever felt unsafe carrying this much cash at one time because within two to three hours it would all be spent.

The money that came in also went on an epic journey. First a generous donor clicked on the GoFundMe link and made a monetary donation via credit card. In two to five

---

[18] GDP Per Capita: Zambia, World Bank accounts data and OECD National Accounts data files 2022

days this money could be accessed by a third party in the US who charged a management fee. Keep in mind that Dora, as a black Zambian woman, is still not allowed to have her own page and receive donations. This third party then transfers the money to Zambia where again a fee for bank transfers and currency exchange is taken out. The money is then received by Footprints of Hope NGO where Dora's lawyer siphons off the amount needed to pay taxes. Finally, approximately a week after a donation is made, the money lands in an account Dora can access. This fractional amount would then evaporate as quickly as it had materialized. Dora was never jaded by this process; she focused rather on the people she feels so compelled to help. "The people that donate are just like me, they are kind. They see something that calls them to help." She explained the relationship between herself and the donors so simply, yet I wondered if the donors knew that's how she saw them. She felt they were one and the same.

Driving down the narrow one-way street through Kamwala market, a self-appointed parking attendant jumped in front of our moving car. Bringing the car to a crawl, I quickly realized what role he was trying to play. He wore a dirty white Adidas t-shirt. Looking at me through the windshield he called out loudly, "Yes boss, parking! Follow me!" The road ahead offered little choice, so I reluctantly followed, trying to ignore him as he waved me forward while running ahead. We pulled into a spot as he directed. As I exited the car he assured me he would be "security boss." Of the many unnecessary services I was routinely offered in Zambia, I actually appreciated these guys. The five to ten kwacha it cost usually felt like money well spent. That is, if they didn't break into your car themselves.

Dora led the way into a large fabric warehouse. Customers spilled out of the front door and loud electric fans buzzed overhead, pushing the stuffy air around the room. Dora jockeyed her way to the front, easing past others and politely pushing back when necessary. This art of weaving through a crowd with ease was something I watched Zambian women do in just about every public space I visited. I wondered if Zambian mothers teach their daughters this skill or if it is in their blood. I stood a few paces back. Thanks to my height, I was still able to perfectly see and hear Dora. Although muscular, Zambian people are rarely tall, which always played to my advantage in markets.

"Can I get the gray uniform fabric?" Dora asked the attendant.

"What do you mean we have a lot of different grays?" he responded gruffly.

"I run a boarding school in Mkushi!" For simplicity's sake Dora would often reference this city instead of her actual village. "We used the charcoal dark gray, if you remember. I bought six or seven reams of it last time."

The man appeared to be the owner, an older Indian gentleman whom Dora recognized. Seemingly annoyed, he began pulling a few gray samples. A narrow lane between the two of us appeared. Mustering my best Zambian auntie energy, I lunged forward. When I arrived at Dora's side, the man's abrasive attitude melted away. Without the need for a glance between us, I knew it was something Dora and I would talk about later. It was always disheartening to witness such moments.

It brought back memories of events that had occurred months earlier. Dora's car had been smashed in a hit and run accident; working with police she had identified the culprit. The man in question was far from poor, running a transport business with several vehicles in his fleet. When the police apprehended him, instead of paying the fines and costs of damages, he bribed the officers. Dora was then left trying to get compensation on her own. She eventually went up the chain of command and I happened to be with her during two of the meetings with police both in Masansa and then at the district police office. The Masansa police station is no more than a few jail cells and a tiny one-room office. The officer greeted us and repeated my name, "Joseph mmh Joseph," nodding his head in approval. The office was claustrophobic. I had been here on my first day with Dora, following up the proceedings of Nandi's rape case. On this day, despite the cramped room, it seemed airier. No doubt the topic of discussion had impacted my physical and mental appreciation of the space around me.

The police officer we spoke to clearly had been bribed and tripped over his words as he explained himself. "When you're with me their attitudes change so much, they act like there is a bwana or a boss around," Dora told me as we left the office. At the district office we met a more professionally mannered police officer. Dora explained the reason for our visit. "I'm here to follow up on a police report I filed after my car was hit. The man has not paid me and I want to press charges."

"Who are you?" He gestured to me, immediately followed by, "Why are you both together?"

"I'm her driver," I said with a closed mouth smile. This had become my standard answer to a question that was often meant to insinuate I had a hierarchical role in Dora's organization or life. The reaction this response would elicit almost always caused Dora to stifle a laugh. Apart from it being an inside joke, it was also the truth. I almost exclusively drove when the two of us were together. This response was my way of tipping my cap to Dora as the "bwana" of her domain.

I carried the reams of gray fabric to the truck while Dora paid, and then she joined me as I lifted the final one into the bed and closed the tailgate. "That guy was pretty rude, no?" I said, gesturing back to the store with my head. "Ugh yea. And did you see how quickly he changed his attitude when you were with me? Whenever we travel together people are more attentive." It was uncommon for Dora to ruminate on the treatment she receives in public spaces, but she does openly recognize the difficulties they pose. She often told me stories of being mistaken at her own school for a lower-level teacher and not the director because of her age. Grocery store clerks question how she could afford so much food. "'Is all this for a company?' they will ask me," Dora said, recalling these almost weekly occurrences.

This type of profiling isn't just limited to the physical spaces she occupies. Online, Dora is subject to people judging every element of how she runs the organization. Driving out of Lusaka I asked her, "What do you think about the legacy you are creating on TikTok for other young Zambian and African girls?"

"I don't really see it that way. I mean, yes. I know that there are people that say I'm an inspiration or like a saint or whatever, but I'm just Dora. I really want people to see me and just think, That's Dora. Maybe they think my work is really great, but I'm just a person." During our discussions and interviews, I tried to give Dora every chance to be profound or share some deeper meaning, but she always came back with very grounded practical answers. As someone who had spent a lot of time with her, I felt this was in part because she doesn't feel fully seen by many people. To her online community, she is "Dora the incredible mother and teacher" and the "village TikToker." To the teachers, she is their boss and leader, and to the students, she is their rock. Beyond anything, Dora just wants to be understood the way she knows herself. "I would say the reason people feel really compelled by my videos is because I'm really myself and I share my energy and the life I'm living out here. I don't represent Zambia or Africa." I nodded, eyes on the road, as a fleet of large buses zoomed past us. "I really do want to change the lives of the village children. I want people to be kind to one another. But I am also just a normal twenty-nine-year-old."

Dora shares the success and setbacks of her life and work at Footprints of Hope with the world. Her personality, passions, and aspirations for the future are at the mercy of the internet. Despite the term being overused, she truly is genuine. During my extended stays at the school, traveling with her, consuming every piece of content she ever made, and interviewing the people in her life, I have come to one simple conclusion: Every person knows a completely different Dora. Over the course of 2022, I made it my mission to try and understand her from a thousand different angles. My goal was to stitch together a portrait that fully encapsulated her many complexities and dimensions. Dora is honest and shares her real self with everyone she meets. Few understand, however, that this reality is piecemeal. Never does Dora fully reveal who she is to a single person. Only with the summation of these views, perspectives, and opinions of others, did I begin to piece together the woman who sat in the passenger seat beside me. Dora isn't complex or enigmatic; she's guarded. Her past, and the events she witnesses every day, have and continue to mold her into the woman she is. It is this nature that has allowed her to excel in such hazardous environments and has fortified her resilience. The silent strength within herself and the identities as a black African woman, single adoptive mother, and passionate local activist are profound. She has heard the words "couldn't," "shouldn't," and "no" more than most hear in a lifetime. It is only by her grace that she is still willing to plant seeds within others and share that success so openly.

Chapter 15

The students began to flood out of the cafeteria and into the neatly swept sand yard. Classes had finished and it was officially the weekend, the day students would return home and the boarders would settle in for a quieter two days of movies, reading, and games. It was a cacophony of noises and songs as the children diverted to either the main gate or their dormitories. Watching this group of 150 children run and skip through the campus was like watching any group of children this age. It was pure schoolyard chaos and wholly unremarkable if you didn't know the stories and backgrounds the children came from. A group of boarding students quickly enveloped me as I walked to Dora's home. As we approached the smaller gate, Dora's daughters opened it and all five launched into a sprint. Sylvia, the youngest with a head comically large for her tiny body, toddled behind her older sisters. Before turning the corner, I could hear them greet their mother with compliments and words of affirmation.

"Not a bad day, huh!" I said to Dora. It had been a busy day, Dora was up early reading emails and working on social media content. By ten we were on the road running errands, and later we sat together doing interview questions and recording discussions for the book. "It was still too much to do though!" She laughed as I followed her into the kitchen. The small room adorned with pots, spices, and canned goods was warm from the oven. I pulled up a chair and sighed, breathing in the sweet smell of the pumpkin bread she was baking. "Want to talk about the future?" I said with a grin, putting my phone on the center of the table.

"Time for an interview, yes!" she said with a labored smile. The two of us had spent countless hours going over questions, recounting parts of her life, and digging into the past. Despite the trust and friendship we had developed, these interviews could still be prickly. Few people understand the strain of having a person dig into every detail of your past and the minute details of your work performance.

At this stage in the year I had gathered more raw interviews, conversations, and observations than I could ever possibly use.

Instead of being relieved, I could see Dora was on edge. "Are you sure you have enough? What about the time…" and she launched into a story about the first girl she had taught to read during a year-long project she had done while a missionary.

"Yes Dora, how could I forget about her? I think we only talked about that story three times!" I said with a smile, sharply breathing out of my nose as a half laugh.

Pulling out the chair opposite of me she eased herself into it. "Well… what's next?"

I opened the recording app on my phone and pressed record. "Tell me about where Footprints is going."

The biggest shift that had affected the school's future had occurred almost exactly a year earlier. The Zambian government had officially cleared Footprints of Hope to legally house children on campus. For eighty of the 150 students, their quality of life improved overnight. "I was just so relieved. They were finally protected and could just focus on learning." Saying this, Dora's thoughts seemed to be elsewhere, perhaps reliving that first night. For most of these students, it would be the first time they had three meals a day and slept in a bed. There were many triumphs during the journey. Dora had raised over $150,000 dollars, garnered an audience of two million at the time the dormitory was open, and was fundraising for an additional two classrooms to be built. Dora worked to frame these moments for me and relive how she felt and the exact things that transpired. While she continued to build classrooms, playgrounds, and make drastic improvements, she also adopted her youngest daughter, Sylvia. Sylvia was an orphan and at just one and a half years old, was shy and untrusting. Dora was again a parent to a child who was an age she had never dealt with before. It was a unique challenge to have twelve kids and be learning how to parent a toddler. But like all other challenges, Dora went all in on being a good mother to Sylvia and is clearly a natural. The two are often confused as biologically related, something that despite her protestations, makes Dora blush.

Dora was now a full time "influencer," sharing her life and mission online with millions of followers. Of these onlookers, thousands would pledge small donations and send supplies. She was a one-woman show, raising enough money on TikTok to support approximately two hundred people: both students and teaching staff. The students, many of whom were previously malnourished, began to look healthier. They received uniforms and their English began to improve dramatically. Viewers online saw this success and began to applaud the great strides the organization had made from its humble beginnings. Then, during this progress, tragedy struck. A young student suddenly died of malaria. "She was such a sweet young girl and the kids really loved her… She just didn't get help quickly enough. We found out and then the school shut down for three days." The student was pulled from school by her parents. Dora, unaware of the severity of the situation, was not notified. Days later the news of the girl's passing reached the school. Dora shouldered the difficult task of informing her students. "It was really hard to tell them. Our kids, they are very emotional." Dora felt a responsibility to also share the reality of what had occurred with her online community. "I wanted to inform people that this is real and it happens here too… And for me, I had a lot of anger. We have all the resources and everything to help the child. There was no need… I was very angry with the mom because they put their pride or whatever right in front of helping the child. If they just allowed us to… She would still be alive." Dora's guilt over the child's death still remained. It was a treatable death. One that in her mind, she should have prevented.

Sitting at the front of the classroom with her cellphone propped up toward her, Dora recorded a video of herself breaking the news to the children. The children are heard in the background, but the video's focus is on Dora. Watching the events unfold, the viewer is virtually placed within the crowd of children. The camera tilted up toward Dora's face evokes each child sitting on the floor craning their necks up, listening intently to Dora. Within hours, the video had reached millions, striking a chord with many as the reality of village life reverberated through TikTok. The student body and teachers rallied around one another as they set their sights on moving forward. Weeks after this video was recorded, I pulled my blue Toyota Hilux through the gates of Footprints of Hope for the very first time. The students rushed to my car and began jumping up and down as Dora appeared around the corner, her iPhone held at chest height recording the commotion. I was being introduced to Dora and the organization during a new and confusing stage of their journey.

"We are working to get better teachers and help our students grow… Also we are working to build a hospital, because the villagers need access to healthcare." The teaching staff at the school fluctuated greatly over the course of 2022. The rural school had difficulties both attracting and retaining quality teaching staff. "A lot of teachers don't really care about their students and they just want a government job that gives them stability regardless of how hard they work," Dora told me as I prodded about solving the chronic staffing issues. It was a sentiment I heard from other Zambians, not just Dora. Often, when I would begin a line of questioning such as how to solve the problems that Dora was challenged by, I had to be careful. The most obvious solutions were often either not viable or changed the dynamic of her school. "I would consider hiring foreign volunteers, but we also want Zambian teachers… Paying more also will not solve this." She pushed on the table, sliding her chair backward and turning to get a dishtowel. Carefully, Dora removed a piping hot loaf of pumpkin bread and loaded another into the bottom rack.

Dora strives to provide the best education and life she possibly can for the children at Footprints of Hope. Without tangible progress or physical growth, however, her online presence and thus the GoFundMe would likely suffer. Throughout the year, Dora's TikTok views had begun to stagnate along with her follower growth. Although her community had mushroomed to a whopping 3.5 million members, she struggled to get a million views on just one video a month. TikTok's algorithm rewards videos that grab attention and pull people in. This means that if Dora can't maintain the attention she once commanded, people will stop watching. If people stop watching, donations will slow and eventually Footprints of Hope will be in jeopardy. "We are far from financial sustainability. We have plans to buy land and start renting it out to pay for the school, but at this stage we are so reliant on donations." Dora was constantly concerned with their current donation model. Some days I would call her and it was clear she was in a great mood because money had come in that week. That meant projects could proceed and the students were secure for another month. "We have maybe enough for a couple months... I would stop all building and cut way back but... if we had to." When I asked about the financial cost and future of the school, it remained murky and uncertain.

It is difficult to predict the future expansion of Footprints of Hope. Again, Dora has not followed many of the typical organizational norms. It is doubtful she could have received any substantial institutional backing with the cornerstone of her fundraising coming from proposed TikTok videos. She is watching the pioneering of this type of fundraising aid, because she is simply at the forefront making it happen. There is no way to predict how sustainable it will be. There is no way to predict if anyone else can replicate what she is doing and how long they could sustain it. There are others in her organization, like Victor and Thandiwe, who could lead schools in other areas. They have the passion to teach and the vision to help the children and the village around them, but would that be enough to be successful? Could they TikTok fundraise as well? Could the brand of success that Dora is building be enough to support larger expansion? More established international NGOs would have answered those questions among their board members. Multiple meetings and discussions would have taken place and a PowerPoint presentation would have shown the pros and cons and final decisions. While they worked behind computer screens doing this, Dora is teaching, sheltering, and feeding kids. Dora has prioritized helping and building rather than saving. At heart, she is a person of action; online, this translates seamlessly to a content-hungry world. If she had waited, saved, and planned over the long term, Dora feels most of her accomplishments never would have come to fruition. This model of "social media humanitarianism" is a unique cultural and social issue that garners judgment from all sides. When speaking on the ethics of her posting habits, Dora said, "I always think about how the children would potentially look back at their time here. I want them to think of how happy and safe they were with us."

That night we discussed the ethics of sharing stories of children online and even in this book; where the line should be drawn and who should be the person to decide exactly what these parameters were. Currently, Dora acts as the guardian of many of the children at the school. She takes this role extremely seriously and feels she always puts their best interests first. As their guardian, she also is responsible for consenting to whether they could be posted online. This creates a clear conflict of interest if real ethical complaints were ever launched. From our initial meeting and in every subsequent interaction,

Dora's focus was and has always been on the well-being of the children at Footprints of Hope.

While writing this book, I spoke openly to Zambians, expats, and foreigners about the ethics of social media humanitarianism. I have watched and met others that try to use Dora's work at Footprints of Hope as a blueprint to fundraising money for their own organization. Many reach their initial fundraising goals but falter to create meaningful online communities and connections that drive lasting change. "I feel like eighty to eighty-five percent of the people that follow me are genuinely invested in what we are doing... Yes, some of the initial followers probably were just like, Oh I can't believe she lives like that, but now I feel like we have real support." As the number of people who engage in social media humanitarianism increases, it's likely the line of ethical behavior will be toed to a far greater extent than Dora ever has. Over the past decade, Western organizations who use images of poor black Africans (often described as "poverty porn") for fundraising schemes have come under fire.[19] Now, in an increasingly digital age, young people around the world are taking notice of what Dora has done. Some see her as an inspiration and agent of change; some think she has developed a model to commodify the strife

---

[19] Pornography of Poverty: Celebrities' Sexual Appeal at Service to the Poor?. The 2nd International Conference on Future of Social Sciences and Humanities, Shahghasemi, E. 2020

of others. The latter may be interested in bettering their own lives while posing with others. Never has sharing to the world and commodifying voyeurism been so accessible. Concerned parties have good reason to feel uncomfortable about these and other trends. The algorithms that drive our online entertainment prioritize the provocative, and this model creates the opportunity for an ethical race to the bottom.

"Sometimes I get comments like 'you've changed' and 'now you dress so much nicer' and 'oh the kids now have everything they need, that's great!' The reality is the kids do look a ton better. They are being fed well and taken care of. They look plump! That's how they should look. What we are doing is working. We still need donations though because if they stop this all ends." Taking a breath in, Dora said defiantly, "And I dress nicer because I have a house not a hut! I am allowed to live a more comfortable life. I'm not going to pretend to be poor or make the kids dirty to get donations." Whether it was a direct statement at other organizations, TikTokers, or NGOs, Dora has a firm stance on the way she presents her students and organization. The difference between Dora and anyone else trying to do something similar is simply character. Dora's values show through in her actions. She is able to build rapport with others and doesn't stifle negative comments but rather addresses them.

Playing devil's advocate during this discussion was difficult. Dora felt under attack. She was defensive, and for good reason. Many of the videos she posted, out of context or from another party, could and should be judged differently. It was hard for her to hear the criticism of the model she used to garner donations because it felt like a personal assault, or so I assumed. I leaned heavily on her trust that I was a staunch supporter of her mission, despite digging through the arguments of others and dropping them on the table between us.

"I would like people to understand that being poor doesn't equal you being dumb or stupid. It's just... you're ignorant. And ignorance is not stupidity. It's a lack of knowledge. So having them understand that and having them understand that just because you help somebody or just because you're helping these kids in this village, it also doesn't make you better. It just makes you privileged and them less privileged," she said in response to a question of the role she played educating foreigners. "And what do you think your role is in helping others understand this?" I said in a soft tone as our conversation turned from a debate into the aspirations she has of passing on the lessons to her online community. "I feel like I'm more of an intermediary. Because I understand the privilege part. And I also understand the not having money part. Mm hmm. So, I understand the villagers... what they want and need for development and where they come from." She sat more upright in her chair. "And I also understand the people who are giving and what they're expecting to get out of it." "Why do people generally give then?" "Some people give to have, like a sense of fulfillment. And others generally give because they just want to help, no credit or anything. They just care."

It was getting late; the kids would be finishing their movie soon and bedtime was around the corner. Wrapping up our lengthy discussion I asked, "Is there anything the online community has taught you?" "Yeah. It's taught me how ignorant people are in terms of poverty and degrees of poverty. How people view people who are poor." Referring to the online community, Dora said, "They think giving them money one time will solve their problems or like everything will be done. A lot of people don't understand the difference between relief and development."

Nandi and Florence peeked into the kitchen; their movie had concluded and it was time to wash their dinner plates before bed. Sitting back in my chair, I felt the weight of our conversation and the exhaustion of the day. Dora had been awake even earlier and was on the move all day. It was clear that our conversation was far from over but both sides were running out of gas. A habit I had learned early on was to always end each interview with a positive question. "If there's one thing you want the world to know, it would be?" I asked, turning my palms to the ceiling and raising my eyebrows with a smile.

Dora paused, then slowly at first said, "That it doesn't matter where you come from, what your background is." Pausing, then almost like it was rehearsed, she stated, "The world is full of potential and given the right opportunities, like the ones we are trying to give these kids, they can accomplish so much more."

Only a handful of students at Footprints of Hope have been attending classes for over two and half years. If Dora's success is measured by their English aptitude, math, and reading scores it would not be an accurate portrait of what has been accomplished. "Success" is an arbitrary metric outsiders use as a form of objective judgment. What Dora has accomplished cannot be quantified by an exam, evaluation, or observation by an educational institution. The degree of suffering of more than 180 children can be. Dora's success rests not in how many doctors, lawyers, or highly trained professionals exit from this first batch of students. Rather, it is in the strength and love she has fostered among a community and for each child. Most of the students are attending classes for the first time in their lives. Many of them hear their first English conversation at the school. To understand what is happening in Mapapa and the gumption of the woman behind it requires an understanding of the strife and pain of these children. Dora has used the tools available to share these challenges and the challenges of her own online. The goal of the school is to change lives through education and to protect those who are vulnerable. The perceptions of others, regardless of how misguided, matter little to Dora and the students. Changing Mapapa may not change the world, but for each child who walks through the yellow gates of Footprints of Hope, their whole world does change.

Chapter 16

Binoculars pressed firmly to my brow, I watched as thirty-five vultures tore apart the carcass of a zebra. It was late in the afternoon in Zambia's renowned South Luangwa National Park. Setting the binoculars down, I turned off the car and leaned back in my seat. My phone chimed with a WhatsApp notification from Dora. A single picture of Nandi in the back seat of the Toyota Prado appeared on my screen. Dora wrote a short caption just below the photo: "Nandi is going to court today, to put the bad man away!" Nandi was wearing a simple black dress and had colorful beads in her hair. She had gained even more weight since the last time I saw her. The smile on her face looked round and healthy. From the composition of the photo, it was clear Dora had turned while in the driver seat and asked Nandi to smile. Of all the voice memos, text updates, photos, and phone calls, this lopsided image impacted me most.

For Dora, this hearing was a culmination of her persistence, decision making, and unwillingness to accept injustice on behalf of a child she loved. Nandi represented hundreds of other cases that had been overlooked, pushed down, or never even brought to the police. Dora doesn't talk about the students or the work she does in any sort of symbolic way. Each child has a name, a unique story, and a relationship with her. Dora isn't seeing the forest through the trees. She understands each tree that makes up the forest. The knowledge and appreciation of each child fuels her instincts to advocate for them. A victory for one child in a legal battle doesn't change the health, well-being, or injustice done to another. In regard to the so-called "larger effort," these somewhat abstract victories do in fact matter. Without explicitly saying this much, it is displayed clearly in the way Dora works tirelessly for each child. Some had legal battles to wage and others did not. Neglect, forced labor, verbal and physical abuse were rarely brought in front of a judge. The children's stories that were heard by the courts became representative of a larger picture. It meant that court cases that were able to be won, needed to be won. Back at the school, legal victories did little to heal the wounds of children who were unable to comprehend a system of "justice" that allowed these acts to be committed. Dora can see the bigger picture and it matters, but the 150 faces etched into her heart need nurturing and development. Paper victories can only hope to change the future, not the present.

It was hard for me not to be pessimistic. Dora is one woman; surely she can't save every child. For that matter, Nandi was never going to get justice. I was proud of her, for the incredible bravery she showed. An eleven-year-old girl standing in front of a court and recounting her story. Dora had shown extraordinary strength and persistence in ensuring that this court day happened. Today was a testament to her effectiveness outside the bound of Footprints of Hope. Dora wanted to acknowledge the legal win Footprints of Hope was on the verge of. Nandi's stepfather, the man who had abused her for so long, would be going to jail for quite some time. To the Zambian courts, followers online, and community members in Mapapa, this was justice. For Dora, the teachers, me, and most importantly Nandi, it was purely symbolic. Justice was the work being done every day to improve this young girl's life. To provide her with a fighting chance at "normal."

Other parties cared about this little girl too, social workers, police officers, judges, and the online community. Their caring was conditional and Nandi would soon be a case, story, or thirty-second video that would fade. Dora's commitment is much deeper than that. She is guided by a deep maternal instinct to protect these children not for a few hours or days, but for their lifetime. I thought back to the first time I met Nandi. She was frail, afraid, and stuttered heavily when she spoke. We had both arrived at Footprints of Hope the same day. On our second day, Nandi was diagnosed with genital warts and syphilis. At the time it was also believed she likely had contracted HIV. Sitting with Nandi in the car, watching Dora's face that first week, was an experience few will ever have. I saw a young woman reach out, hoping by any means to pull this young girl back into a world of possibilities. Dora shielded Nandi from the reality of what was happening. "You're just sick, that's all," was her go-to line when it came to explaining AIDs or other STIs with the youngest children. It was a softer truth for people far too young to understand the complexities of the acts committed against them.

During those first few days and weeks at the school, a word that stayed in my head was "empathy." Rarely can anyone truly employ empathy for another human being. The act of empathizing requires a unique understanding of the person, their culture, background, and almost mirrorlike situations in both people's lives. Yet, we are supposed to try and employ more empathy in our everyday lives. Being at the school and witnessing everything around me, the idea of empathy was difficult. I couldn't understand what these people were feeling, thinking, anxious about, or emotionally digesting. To try to put myself in their shoes seemed disrespectful, in part because the village kids ran around barefoot. Dora is a teacher. Being the head of an NGO does not come naturally. It's a process of growth and learning she is undertaking as she leads Footprints of Hope. At her core, Dora helps others understand and learn. For the children of Mapapa village, this includes feeding, clothing, housing, and protecting them. To attend school and learn, these necessities of life must be met. To the rest of the world, she shares a lesson in the enormous gaps in education, wealth, social rights, and access to opportunity that exist. She teaches the world that they don't and likely never will fully comprehend the thoughts and emotions of people in a place so distant. Culturally, socially, and politically different is perhaps only appreciated with a more nuanced understanding of Mapapa. But rather than focusing on these important factors of her work, Dora instead preaches kindness.

"What do you see yourself as? If you had to define it, I mean, like, boil it down?" I asked Dora in the hope she would do my job, summating all her parts and responsibilities. Dora emphatically turned to me said, "A human!" She was laughing but sort of frustrated with her silly response. "No no no,

I don't mean like esoterically or like—" She cut me off. "No, I mean a human. An honest to god human! I believe we should all help each other. A human being. What an actual human being should be like. Helping others. That is humanity. That is being kind. That is how I see myself. I don't see it as humanitarian work. I don't see it as aid. I don't see it as whatever... It's humanity, that's honestly who I am." Her smile had faded and a determined look had spread across her face.

At twenty-three, Dora adopted her first daughter. Overnight, she became a guardian and mother to a teenage girl with trauma and autism. Dora didn't and couldn't understand how Veronica felt, or the emotions of the young girl standing in her doorway. "It was a Tuesday morning and here was this girl asking to do my laundry... I didn't feel like I had a choice, I had to help," she said. Dora's maternal instinct and deep need to help vulnerable people didn't manifest itself in a single day. Outside of her home, she found herself surrounded by doubt and negative voices. She lived through trauma at the hands of others and was cast off as a liar. Despite every pressure, opportunity, and excuse she had to let her well of kindness dry up, she wouldn't. Dora's love to teach is an expression of her desire to care for others. To plant within them both encouragement and love that she herself so often felt without. Stories of her acts of kindness and expressions of love abound. "I have felt very alone a lot of my life and I didn't have support at so many points, like anyone," Dora said as she thought out loud toward the end of a long car ride. This absence of encouragement and prolonged feeling of loneliness also highlighted the moments she did feel love. Moments when Ashley, Thandiwe, her grandmother, and others stepped up and reminded her of the love the world did have to offer.

For the children at Footprints of Hope, Dora is more than a teacher. She is not the head of an NGO. She's not a public servant or an authority to fear. To the children from the ages of three to fifteen, Teacher Dora embodies kindness and warmth in their lives. For some of the children with functional families, she is a loving aunt or mentor. To the children who were wilting away unnoticed, Dora is a mother, a supporter, and their caretaker. Dora was a young woman waiting for something to pour her entire heart into, whether that was a family, project, or community. In more ways than one, Footprints of Hope has become all three. The teachers, students, caretakers, and surrounding community are a family. The community has its ups and downs, struggles, and issues. The bond the students, staff, and Dora share supersedes those and enables them to have an incredible future despite their past and at times uncertain future.

While I observed Dora closely for many months, she always

told me, "I'm not all holy," and "I can actually be very mean sometimes… I wonder if I am a legitimately kind person sometimes." The internet and news outlets cast the best light on both her mission and Dora as a person. Reading those articles, watching her content, and hearing others explain her as a woman are highly complementary. Dora, a self-described "human" like all of us, is prone to many faults. Working closely with her, I found her greatest faults to be rooted in deep insecurity. It was not hard to hypothesize as to the origin of those insecurities. She has accomplished so much in the eyes of her community both online and locally, along with proving her most ardent detractors wrong. Yet, her insecurities remain.

Asking about them proved difficult. She was more open about wanting a family and seeking out a partner. When it came to discussing her dyslexia, I found a more closed-off Dora than I had encountered any other time. Her dyslexia and absence of a romantic relationship cut deep into her psyche. Dora was adamant throughout the interview process that I highlight her flaws, not paint her as she said, "In a way that makes people think I'm super special or amazing. Like other people can do these things. I'm not magical or anything." Her struggles when it came to grappling with her dyslexia, however, were essential in telling the greater story of her achievements. Dora had described CELTA and DELTA as "Hell on earth."

How was I to communicate the personal difficulty and her accomplishment in overcoming those challenges without sharing this information? Dora adamantly preached that "poor people are not dumb, they are ignorant… they don't have the same educational opportunities." This view seemed to be at odds with the fact that she herself had trouble separating her own academic ability from her intelligence.

The woman who so often sat across from me sharing news highlights, science facts, and trivia is highly intelligent. This is clear to both strangers and people intimately involved in her life. Hiding her shortcomings only does Dora a disservice, which is to ignore the full scope of the challenges she faced throughout her life. It is her innate humanness in having flaws and being self-conscious that makes Dora the woman she is. Those who look up to Dora need to be bolstered by not only her incredible strength, intelligence, and kindness, but also her flaws. Dora was and is at times cranky, excited, loud, frustrated, mean, authoritative, and confused, all of which could occur in the same day. It was Dora who was privately trying to define exactly who she was. I and those around her had accepted she could never be simply wrapped up into a model for others. It is this that makes her most compelling.

Despite her intelligence and broad life experience, Dora's decision to move to Mapapa as an outsider ignored all logic.

In hindsight, it took enormous faith and a spirited will that could not be quelled by others. "Even if I just had one classroom and helped teach village kids that was okay... I was fine being *Little House on the Prairie*," she told me, harking back to the days in a mud hut. As she cooked popcorn over a fire and enticed her first students to sit through a lesson, her unwavering dream began to take shape. The incredible rise Dora and her organization have had on social media has brought a period of growth and prosperity. For many of the children, 2022 marked the first year of living in a safe home with three meals a day for an entire year. Footprints of Hope has only had an operational dormitory for 50 percent of its history. The future of the children relies totally on Dora's ability to continue to fundraise and provide for the school. The struggle between highlighting the school's growing successes and yet a sustained need for donations without groveling is a social media question Dora grapples with each day.

Every new student that passes through the yellow metal gates at Footprints of Hope unknowingly opens themselves to a new world of opportunities. Dora's incredible efforts have worked so well that villagers assumed she was a satanist. Villagers reasoned how else could a single mother feed, clothe, and educate so many poor children. It was the unending spirit of a woman dedicated to chipping away at the inequalities and suffering thrust upon her country's most vulnerable group. Dora's ability to sympathize with their struggles and communicate broadly the need to pull these children into a land of opportunity has inspired millions. For the children of Mapapa, Dora is a much simpler character, one they love and share a deep gratitude for. Dora who asks for nothing in return, and that has raised both questions from villagers and intrigue from around the world. It is thanks to her and the thousands who donated and continue to do so that these children for the first time in their lives have a stable diet, education, and emotional support network of teachers and caretakers. Dora, a young woman who started with a dream, a cell phone, and a mud hut, is now ushering the youngest generation of Zambian villagers to a brighter future.

Postscript

In 1839 the first non-governmental organization was established, The Anti-Slavery Society. Its American founders likely didn't understand the enormous impact the organizational structure they devised would have on the world. The modern NGO varies greatly from these modest beginnings; however, those renegade abolitionists are remembered most prominently by Fredrick Douglas, who paved the way for future generations. [20]

The exact number of NGOs operating throughout the African continent is unknown. In 2015 it was reported that South Africa alone had over 140,000 registered NGOs.[21] The

[20] The Rise and Rise of NGOs - Global Policy Forum, Public Services International, Peter Hall Jones, May 2006

[21] NGOs today: Competing for resources, power and agency, Mail &

proliferation of "do-gooders," as they are often seen by locals, is a complex subject of debate. Zambia was previously home to the largest cohort of Peace Corps volunteers and is a hub for many missionaries across the African continent.[22] Many of these groups and people do extraordinary work and strive to act ethically. There are likely an equal number that stifle local economic growth and source donations through marketing schemes propped up on tropes of poor black Africans.

Living in Zambia, it's hard not to recognize the enormous impact AID organizations, NGOs, and missionaries have on the country. During the time I spent in Lusaka, I met just about every type of expat. Missionaries, foreign bureaucrats, oil and mining employees, and volunteers who had come to "help." I myself was on a US government grant, of which my express purpose was to provide data to the Zambian Department of National Parks on the economic impact of ecotourism. The only objective I needed to complete in the eyes of my government, however, was to be a "goodwill ambassador." I took solace in the fact that a rigorous process was undertaken to be selected, elevating me from some "do-gooder" to a person with legitimate expertise. It's why, despite some of my apprehension, I personally see great value for both the host nation

---

Guardian, Kentse Radebe & Ncedisa Nkonyeni March, 2020

[22] An inside look a the return of Peace Corps Volunteers to Zambia, Peace Corp.Gov, Gina Althoff March 2022

and the United States of America to engage in the Fulbright program. Despite this feeling, I knew any judgmental shots that I aimed at these expats could also be leveled at me. I too played a role in this larger scheme. These and other thoughts were in my mind prior to writing this book.

Before I began writing, the entire process was brought to a head with one critical question: why? It was a question I could answer in a heartbeat, and for that reason, I felt compelled to proceed. Family and friends were upfront about the fact that judgment and perhaps criticism would arise. I was, after all, going into a remote area to write about a black Zambian woman who raised funds via social media. I, a tall white male from the other side of the world, differ greatly from Dora. I acknowledged these sentiments but felt that because my focus was and is on raising the platform on which Dora stands, it was worth pursuing. For Dora, having a book written about her was not only an opportunity to raise awareness but also to increase donations.

When we first sat down to discuss the book, we were both nervous and excited about its potential. As we began the interview and shadowing process, her insecurities slowly began to reveal themselves. We were a team of chance and circumstance. Logistically, the interview and writing process started almost immediately after our first discussion about writing the book. The story, however, took much greater shape over the following months. Most days were quite slow, waking up at 6 a.m., writing and waiting for Dora to be ready at 10 a.m. to start our day. During those hours, Dora would connect with parents and catch up on the previous day's work. Dora worked to provide access to many people in her life, and slowly we began to trust one another. Without the internet and largely disconnected from the outside world, it was easy to feel isolated, a feeling Dora was clearly all too familiar with. As the first months passed by, Dora began to relax, as did I.

As a writer, I knew it was important to share Dora's level of education with readers. Her achievements are impressive, in large part because of the challenges she was forced to overcome. To Dora, however, speaking openly about this seemed counterintuitive. Dora is extremely proud of her high school and teaching degree. Every time I tried to have a discussion about the reading, writing, and comprehension level she and others with a similar education had attained, she was closed off. "Elite" was her description of the schools she had attended. Speaking with other educated Zambians, and her friends and extended network, I learned that we had differing perspectives on what an elite education is. It was one of many moments when I was reminded of just how different our lives and worlds are. Dora was correct in saying the schools she attended were elite. Compared to a public education in Zambia, her primary and secondary school were above the fold. In a global context, this was not the case. This was made most apparent by Dora's need to improve her writing skills as she rose within the missionary organizations. When she told me about that time in her life, it was hard not to be inspired. She was a young woman who had done all the right things but was being shut out by others. That part of her journey was not only compelling but also showed her tenacious thirst to better herself. Ignoring her own ego and reassessing her academic ability took real courage.

While working together there were many tough questions to be answered. An NGO funded on social media relevance was bound to have many legitimate pitfalls. When I pressed her on these issues and claims of internet detractors, I found she took those sorts of allegations very personally. Footprints of Hope is so tightly interwoven with Dora that she truly is the embodiment of the NGO. She was open about this issue and is working to change it, trying to pave a sustainable path forward for Footprints of Hope separate from her own likeness. Despite this, it was still difficult for her to see the questions as purely interview topics, many of which I felt readers were justified in asking. The model of funding Dora has mastered is likely to be a roadmap for others.

In practice, Dora navigates the practical issues of a social media–funded NGO extremely well. Dealing with donors, keeping a clean image, fundraising appropriately, paying taxes, and always providing financial transparency. She struggled, however, to structure a coherent rebuttal to many of the questions aimed at the fundraising model she uses, in large part because she herself is the determining factor. Why Footprints of Hope is an ethical and well-run organization comes down to Dora. Her personal decisions and leadership are key. Detractors can only level claims against her funding model; they have little ammunition against Dora herself. As someone both close to Dora and viewing her organization as an outsider, I saw both sides. Dora is and was acting with integrity. However, it is not hard to imagine others copying her model and being less than honest. In some ways she was laying a blueprint for others to follow. However, the actions of others are not at all her responsibility, although they could impact her negatively, the aftermath of an NGO scam or other bad actors making people less likely to donate to an ethically run organization. As our relationship deepened, I began to see the wholeness of Dora and her NGO. It was only as I became more aware of Dora that we could share the greater workings of her organization with readers.

Through hours of interviews, shadowing, and speaking

with her extended network, the real story behind Footprints of Hope emerged. Dora showed great patience and trust in me as a writer, which I will forever be grateful for. Ultimately, the process of writing this book and becoming intimately aware of the ongoing events at Footprints of Hope raised many more questions about foreign aid, education, and Zambian representation within their own domestic affairs. At times I was frustrated; it was during those times that my true passion for this book and story was most evident. All of the events in this story are true. The names of the children were changed, to protect their identities. At Footprints of Hope I was reminded of the incredible power that one person can have on generations of people. Dora is giving the most valuable gift to the children of Mapapa: an education. This is their chance at becoming more than what they and others have thought was possible. It was an honor to watch them grow and learn. This book will remain part of their legacy, and Dora's, as future students pass through the school and go on to achieve marvelous things.

Acknowledgments

Thank you to my immediate family, who have been a deep source of inspiration and motivation throughout this process. To my parents, Jill and Bryan, thank you for reading the first draft and assisting throughout the editing process. To Angela, my best friend and sister, thank you for pushing me to do more and exceed my own expectations. To my brother, Sam, thank you for your encouragement and lightheartedness during our late night phone calls. To Elizabeth, my older sister, thank you for all of the advice and incredible research support over the past two years.

Thank you to Dora Moono Nyambe. Your strength and tenacity have inspired me and will continue to inspire others for generations to come. I am extremely proud of you and know that this is just the beginning.

Thank you to Johanna Vierinkari and Clara Rice. Clara, thank you for being a wonderful friend and generous host. Johanna, thank you for the great friendship and loyalty you showed me throughout the year. During some of the most stressful times your friendship and kindness meant the most to me.

Thank you to Sophia Zhang and Norah Justinger. Sophia, I want to thank you for all the emails written, phone calls made, and time spent connecting with others. Norah, thank you for all the work in creating meaningful graphics and content. I wish you both all the best as you head to university.

Thank you to Teacher Thandiwe and Teacher Victor for being valued friends and supporters of the book. Teacher Thandiwe, I will miss your wonderful sense of humor and ability to see the light in dark places. It was an absolute honor to see you become a mother and meet your son. Teacher Victor, I want to thank you for your friendship and insight. I know that you will continue to be an invaluable role model for all the young boys at the school.

Thank you to the teachers at Footprints of Hope and all the friends, family members, and staff that made me feel at home while at the school. The lengths you took to ensure I was a member of the team were not unnoticed. I look forward to seeing you all in the future!

Thank you to my grandparents, Jim and Joann Shea and Joan and Thomas Schmitt. To Joann Shea, thank you for always believing in me and boosting my self-confidence. To Jim Shea, I feel so lucky to have fostered such a meaningful relationship with you through our mutual love of reading. To Joan Schmitt, thank you for always encouraging me to be adventurous and vocalizing your support. To the late Thomas Schmitt, I know you would be extremely proud of our entire family; you are greatly missed.

To all my Tiktok and social media supporters, thank you for being there for every step of the journey. The encouragement, love, and curiosity you shared inspired me to be the best I could be. I'm proud of what we have accomplished as a community and look forward to many more adventures together.

Launch Team Acknowledgments

Thank you to our launch team, for supporting this project and sharing this story with the world!

Abhijith Suboyin

Albert Basse IV

Abrahim Elset

Amy Reiter

Ben Seigel

Blake Hishmeh

Cally Silberbauer

Chelsea Stafford

Kayla Porupsky

Kristi Takens

Liesse Ella Van Der Velden

LuAnn Baker

Lulwerki Shmay

Maggie O'Brien

Matthew Poblador

Marin Reed

Crispin Ferris

Daizane Hauge

Dora Loczy

DJ Kullas

Ashley Bianchimano

Erick Monroy

Elena Austras

Emily Schultz

Emily Wallace

Gaisva Pranaityte

Jephte Alphonse

Julia McCarthy

Jacob Lillelund

Jojo Green

Maya Kilshaw

Mulemba Ndonji

Noud Goossens

Rahel Yirdaw Girmay

Rozemarijn Reinieren

Robert Bachmann

Sabrina Reese

Skyler Nasrallah

Soni Cido

Taraz Mahony

Tommy Clark

Tommy Harte

Victoria Lord

Zakiyyah Lulat

Stay Connected

Joseph Schmitt

Tiktok: @explorewithjoe

Instagram:

@explorewithjoe_official

Website:

josephjamesschmitt.com

Dora Moono Nyambe

Tiktok: @doramoononyambe

Instagram:

@doramoononyambe

Website:

footprintsofhope.net

The future of Footprints of Hope relies on your donations, please visit Dora's social media pages to donate today!

www.underazambiantree.com

underazambiantree@gmail.com

Joseph Schmitt is an American writer, ecotourism researcher, and expedition traveler. He was born and raised in Wisconsin before attending Northeastern University in Boston, Massachusetts. Joseph was awarded the prestigious Fulbright Research Grant to conduct ecotourism research in Zambia. Today, he continues to conduct research, write, and seek adventure.

Made in the USA
Monee, IL
28 March 2023